P9-AGX-041

Also by

JOSEPH HELLER

CATCH-22

We Bombed in New Haven

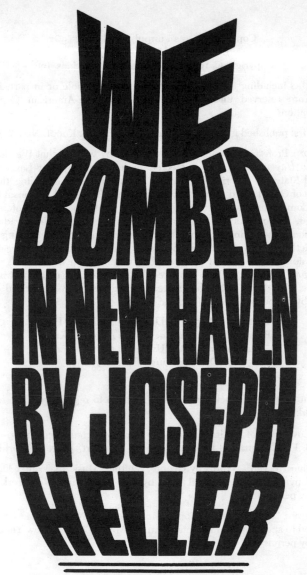

WE BOMBED IN NEW HAVEN

BY JOSEPH HELLER

A DELTA BOOK

Copyright © as an unpublished work 1967
by Scapegoat Productions, Inc.
Copyright © 1967 by Scapegoat Productions, Inc.

All rights including the right of reproduction in whole or in part, in any form, are reserved under International and Pan-American Copyright Conventions.

First published in the United States by Alfred A. Knopf, New York

CAUTION: Professionals and amateurs are hereby warned that *We Bombed in New Haven*, being fully protected under the Copyright Laws of the United States of America, the British Commonwealth, including the Dominion of Canada, and all other countries of the Berne and Universal Copyright Conventions, is subject to royalty. All rights, including professional, amateur, motion picture, recitation, lecturing, public reading, radio and television broadcasting, and the rights of translation into foreign languages, are strictly reserved. Particular emphasis is laid on the question of readings, permission for which must be secured in writing from the author's agent: Scapegoat Productions, Inc., c/o Greenbaum, Wolff & Ernst, 437 Madison Avenue, New York, N.Y. The amateur acting rights are controlled exclusively by Scapegoat Productions, Inc.

Delta ® TM 755118, Dell Publishing Co., Inc.
Reprinted by arrangement with Alfred A. Knopf
Manufactured in the United States of America
First Delta Printing—February, 1969

The author gratefully acknowledges permission to reprint from the following works:

"The Love Song of J. Alfred Prufrock" from *Collected Poems 1909–1962*, by T.S. Eliot. Reprinted by permission of Harcourt, Brace & World, Inc.

"My Blue Heaven"—Words by George Whiting, Music by Walter Donaldson. Copyright 1927, renewed 1955 by Leo Feist, Inc., New York, N.Y. Used by permission.

Parody on: "Roll Me Over" Copyright 1944 by J. Norris Music Co. Ltd., assigned to and copyright by Peter Maurice Music Co. Inc., New York, N.Y. Used by permission.

TO JOE STEIN

Who encouraged and helped me

We Bombed in New Haven

Characters

.

THE MAJOR

CAPTAIN STARKEY

SERGEANT HENDERSON

CORPORAL BAILEY

CORPORAL SINCLAIR

PFC. JOE CARSON

PRIVATE FISHER

SOME IDIOTS
(Not less than two, not more than five)

RUTH
(A Red Cross worker)

TWO SPORTSMEN:
A HUNTER A GOLFER

YOUNG FISHER
(Fisher's kid brother)

STARKEY'S SON

The Time: Always the present, the exact day and hour at which the play is being performed.

The Place: The theater, city, and country in which the play is presented.

Production at different times and in different cities, as well as changes in the actors playing the roles, may require a number of changes in place names and dialogue for certain of the lines to remain meaningful.

.

ACT
One

O O O O O O O

THE SETTING on stage is of an ordinary American Air Force briefing room in a bungalow in a war somewhere.

Even before the house lights have been fully dimmed, there is the noise of heavy objects being moved about on stage in back of the curtain. The curtain starts to rise; it jerks to a stop about half-way up, as though jamming by accident, or as though the person in control of the curtain has just realized it has been lifted a few minutes prematurely, for all of the stage scenery has not yet been put in place.

The premature lifting of the curtain has exposed about seven or eight airmen, dressed in flight suits and parachute harnesses, in the act of moving props and parts of the set out on stage into proper position. One by one they stop with looks of surprise and intense embarrassment at the realization that they are now in view of the audience. They stare helplessly, as though powerless to decide what to do next. A dull, even light falls over everything, for

3

the correct illumination for the play has not yet
been adjusted, either.

The briefing room is composed of three separate
areas. One, on a slightly raised platform, is the
main briefing section; it serves also as the Major's
office and contains a long, large work table, or
desk, and several chairs. There is a blackboard on
one wall and layers of maps, some on rollers, on another. There is a large globe in a floor stand near
the corner of the desk. Written in chalk on the
blackboard are columns of names that include those
of most of the characters in the play, as well as the
true surnames of many of the people connected
with the actual production.

When the curtain rises, the Major is sitting at
the desk with a sullen and preoccupied expression,
working intently over a manuscript that might (or
might not) be the script of the same play that is
now being performed. He is a somber, imposing
man in his fifties, and his enigmatic poise and self-
confidence suggest a knowledge and authority that
are ominous and inscrutable.

The second part of the briefing room is the general assembly area, in which most of the indoor
action by the men will take place. It is almost a
room apart from the area in which the Major is
working. It contains a window, some benches, and
a number of short sections of joined seats and
desks, similar to those found in children's school-
rooms, although these, rather than arranged in
rows, stand around in a haphazard lack of design,
as though exactly as left by the last people to use
them. One section of two joined chairs has actually been tipped over and left lying on the floor. On

one of the walls is a large sign that says "NO SMOK-
ING." A few of the men were working in this area
to create this disorderly effect when the curtain
started up and brought them to a halt. And at least
one of them is smoking. Throughout the play, the
enlisted men will light cigarettes whenever they
are alone, extinguish them quickly when one of the
two officers appears.

The premature lifting of the curtain has also
caught Captain Starkey in the process of entering
and crossing through this area toward the Major.
Starkey is a man in his forties, and he is smoking a
slim cigar with an air that is placid and slightly
jaunty. He carries a brown leather portfolio and a
folded copy of *The New York Times* (or of the
local newspaper that would be most easily recog-
nized by the audience), and he is moving across
the stage toward the Major in much the same self-
assured manner of any well-placed civilian execu-
tive reporting for his day's or evening's work. He
stops instantly with a look of sharp amazement
when he discovers that he is already in view of the
audience, obviously a few minutes earlier than he
had expected. His first reaction is to remove the
cigar from his mouth, as though to hide it, and he
looks about in confusion.

The third section of the briefing room is the clear
area connecting the other two. It is bordered in the
back by the wall of the building, which contains the
doorway, some windows, some posters, and a bul-
letin board. It is mainly this part of the stage set
that has not yet been put in place.

Flustered and awkward, all the men on stage
stand gazing at Starkey, as though awaiting in-

structions. Starkey surveys the mishap glumly; he
looks at the men, the half-raised curtain, the observ-
ing audience, and he frowns with annoyance at the
realization that something has gone wrong with
things from the very beginning. He mutters to himself disconsolately and then calls out politely to the
Major.

STARKEY

Oh, Jesus. Major?
(The Major looks up from his work and studies the
situation with a glower of severe displeasure. He
glances at his watch, ponders a few seconds, and
then nods curtly, giving a signal that Starkey in-
terprets immediately)
Okay, men! Get back to work! Finish it up—fast, fast!
(The men respond hurriedly and resume toiling
with the flats and props that will constitute the com-
pleted set. As Starkey watches, they slide the re-
maining sections of wall where they belong, make
a few final adjustments with the windows, posters,
and chairs, and then vanish through the door or out
into the wings by darting in front of the scenery.
Satisfied, Starkey resumes walking calmly across
stage to the Major's desk, still uncertain what to
do with his cigar. With a sidelong glance at the
audience, he crushes it out finally and lets it fall into
a wastebasket. He takes a corner of the desk for his
own use. He puts the newspaper down and starts
to unzip his portfolio. The curtain starts moving
again and opens fully, the lights adjust to throw the
brightest illumination on Starkey and the Major,
and the play proper begins.
The Major continues working in silence over the

6

open manuscript before him, copying passages on the top page of a yellow pad. His desk is a litter of maps, documents, and ornamental objects that serve as toys or paperweights. These include miniatures of the Eiffel Tower, the leaning tower of Pisa, the Empire State Building; there are three billiard balls on the desk, some sets of colorful toy soldiers in the uniforms of imperial fighters of another age, a few upright missiles on their launching pads, and several pieces of conventional cannon. There is a glossy souvenir Pan American jet airliner, a hand grenade, and a 37-millimeter shell.

While the Major writes, Starkey removes a clipboard from his portfolio and then a silver whistle attached to a cord that he slips around his neck. He drifts casually to the wall containing the maps and rolls one down. It is a map of the world.

A large clock in the briefing room keeps actual time accurately throughout the play)

Well, Major? Where are they going today?

MAJOR

Constantinople.

(Starkey takes a puzzled second glance at the wall map)

STARKEY

There is no Constantinople. It's Istanbul now.

MAJOR

I know that.

STARKEY

Then why are we going there?

7

MAJOR

We're not going there. They are.

STARKEY

Why are *they* going there?

MAJOR

(Tapping his manuscript)
Because it says so.

STARKEY

Is it dangerous?

MAJOR

Not for those who survive. For those who don't—well, I'd
call that dangerous.

STARKEY

Will anybody be killed there?
(The Major nods)
And we just go on working. If somebody's going to die
today, why must it be over something that doesn't even
exist, like Constantinople? Why don't we at least call it
Istanbul? At least *that's* a name worth dying for.

MAJOR

It says Constantinople.

STARKEY

Can I ask a question?

MAJOR

(With a slight smile)
You are.

STARKEY

I'm a pretty easy-going guy, Major. I think you know that. I don't complain, and I do everything I'm told, and all in all I know I have a pretty soft time of it here. *And* I have the second prettiest girl on the base, who is also pretty soft. But every now and then I think I do want to ask a question. May I? Who's in charge here?

MAJOR

I am.

STARKEY

No. Who's the boss? Who's running the show?

MAJOR

I am.

STARKEY

The whole show. Who is the person who tells you to tell me to tell them that they've got to go today to—God help me!—*Constantinople?*

MAJOR

The colonel.

STARKEY

Who tells the colonel? I know—the general. Major, let me in on the biggest military secret of all. Who's really in charge and who's really responsible?

(Instead of replying, the Major smiles slightly again, looks at the clock on the wall, then at his wrist watch)

MAJOR

What time is it?

9

STARKEY

(Sighs with disappointment)
Do you want the men?

(The Major tears from the pad the sheet of paper
on which he has been writing and hands it to
Starkey, who affixes it to his clipboard)

MAJOR

Yes. There's work to be done.

STARKEY

I'll get them.
(Blows his whistle shrilly to summon the men)
There'll be time. Yes . . . I think . . .

(Carrying his clipboard, Starkey walks leisurely
into the assembly area, talking without pause, reciting formally the lines that follow. The door
opens and the men begin filing in, carrying map
cases and flight kits and wearing combat uniforms.
They include the same men we saw earlier placing
the scenery. They move toward the chairs and
benches, some kidding with each other noisily,
some very serious.

   Henderson, a young sergeant, seems the most
confident and discerning, and there is a cocky self-
assurance about him as he saunters forward that
suggests a vain and mocking arrogance. Bailey, a
well-built corporal, is a few years older than Henderson; he is something of a clown and athlete
who is susceptible to sudden silences and sudden
changes of temperament. Sinclair, another corporal, is surly and pulls away angrily when one of the
others tries playfully to jostle with him. Fisher, a

private, is the youngest and seems earnest, naïve, and polite. All of these are young, about thirty or under.

The oldest of the others who enter is Pfc. Joe Carson, a career soldier almost ready for retirement, which puts his age near sixty. Service stripes indicating length of service form a long row up his arm and contrast with the single insignificant stripe designating his rank. He is, all in all, a soft, somewhat stupefied old man of a different era who seems to have neither affinity nor affection for any of the younger men in the group of soldiers of which he is a part. He is frequently puzzled by many of the things the others discuss, and he has the surprising habit of bursting pleasurably into song whenever a cue presents itself.

The five other men who comprise the group are as silent and slow as idiots; in fact, they *are* Idiots. With sparse exceptions, these Idiots will utter no sounds throughout the play, and there is something vaguely oafish and wooden about their movements as they join in with the others to obey the same orders and go through the same actions with the same willingness and competence.

Captain Starkey, who is reciting his lines without interruption, and with considerable self-satisfaction, speaks first to the men as they enter and then directly to the audience. The Major continues studying his manuscript, turning a page every few seconds as though reading along with the spoken words, and glancing up from time to time to observe the others.

Henderson, instead of following the others to the benches and chairs, moves toward Starkey with a

contemptuous smirk and stands waiting beside him
as Starkey concludes his recitation to the audience
with a proud flourish)

STARKEY

".............................. there will be time
To prepare a face to meet the faces that you meet;
There will be time to murder and create,
And time for all the works and days of hands
That lift and drop a question on your plate;
Time for you and time for me,
And time yet for a hundred indecisions,
And for a hundred visions and revisions
Before the taking of a toast and tea."

HENDERSON

(Mimicking scornfully)
"Before the taking of a toast and tea."
    (Speaking with the same scorn)
Captain, that's T. S. Eliot you're doing, not Henry Wads-
worth Longfellow.
    (Reciting with a delicacy and irony more appropri-
    ate to the line)
"Before the taking of a toast and tea."

STARKEY

(Dryly)
Thank you, Sergeant Henderson. It's a pleasure to be in-
structed by someone of your extensive training and educa-
tion.

HENDERSON

(With equal sarcasm)
Don't mention it, Captain Starkey. It's a pleasure to be of
help, sir, to someone who needs it so badly.

(The men laugh at Henderson's rejoinder. Surprisingly, Starkey frowns with only mild annoyance at this impertinence. He consults his clipboard, and his manner tightens and becomes more military)

STARKEY

Okay, we'll begin now. Let's see who's here.

(Comically, Bailey takes a few giant goosesteps forward, clicks his heels, and delivers a massive salute, grossly exaggerating each movement)

BAILEY

Corporal Rudolph Bailey, sir, reporting for duty as ordered, sir, and ready, willing, and able to go into action, sir.

(Starkey gives him a long look of displeasure. Bailey finally wilts beneath Starkey's gaze and shifts uneasily)

Don't you want me to do that?

STARKEY

No.

(Bailey shrugs and steps back. Starkey frowns at him a moment longer, then advances to begin calling the roll)

Sergeant Henderson.

(Henderson, in contrast to his earlier manner of flippant disdain, snaps to attention and answers smartly)

HENDERSON

Here, sir!

STARKEY

Corporal Bailey.

13

BAILEY

Here, sir!

STARKEY

Corporal Sinclair.

> (There is silence, defiant silence, from Sinclair. He
> is directly in front of Starkey, and the two men
> glare at each other, their faces only inches apart.
> The idiot nearest Sinclair nudges him; Sinclair
> jabs back at him furiously)

Sinclair!

> (Sinclair still refuses to answer and Starkey shouts
> still louder)

Can't you hear me?

SINCLAIR

> (Shouting back at him)

Can't you see me?

STARKEY

Why don't you answer "present" when you hear me calling your name?

SINCLAIR

Why don't you *mark* me "present" if you see me standing here?

> (Paces a step or two in anger)

You dumb son of a bitch!

STARKEY

> (Defensively)

I've got to call the roll, that's why! I've got this list to read! I've got my instructions to follow, too! Are you here or aren't you?

(Sinclair sighs wearily, as though unable to believe the question, or the situation, and maintains a silence for a few seconds, while Starkey still stares at him, inches away, and glowers)

SINCLAIR

(Finally)
I am here, *sir*.

STARKEY

Thank *you*. Private First Class Joe Carson.

JOE

Here, sir.

STARKEY

Private Harry Fisher.

FISHER

Present, sir.

STARKEY

Good. All you men present and accounted for. And you five idiots? One, two, three, four, five. Fine. Let's go ahead.

(Starkey's manner turns airy and congenial as he moves into a position to read to the men from the sheet the Major has just given him. His voice is almost hearty, and there is a strong suggestion in the banter that follows that he is getting most of his lines from the sheet on his clipboard)
Greetings, boys. From the Major, from me, and from the President of the United States. You are all hereby ordered . . . to a war.

(The men stir and murmur and applaud and then
break out with a few short exclamations of disdain
before their separate comments emerge)

HENDERSON

So that's what it is. A war.

STARKEY

Indeed it is.

SINCLAIR

And Uncle Sam wants me.

STARKEY

Indeed he does. So now you know what we're doing here.
All of us—all of *you*—are fighting a war. And the target
for today is—
    (Smiles and shakes his head in disbelief)
—somebody ask me what the target for today is.

(Fisher rises to comply, while Henderson makes a
contemptuous kissing noise to ridicule and embar-
rass him)

FISHER

Sir?
    (Fisher breaks off to throw Henderson a dirty look,
    then begins again)
Sir? What's the target for today?

STARKEY

Bailey, you wouldn't believe it.

FISHER

I'm Fisher, sir.

STARKEY

Fisher, *you* wouldn't believe it, either.

HENDERSON

Henderson would believe it.
   (Pauses to build up suspense for his joke)
Bismarck, North Dakota.

STARKEY

No. Constantinople.

   (The men are astonished)

FISHER

Sir?

BAILEY

Well, I'll be damned!

JOE

   (Scratching his head)
Where's that?

HENDERSON

Don't any of you bright people up on top know—

STARKEY

We know.

HENDERSON

It's Istanbul, now.

STARKEY

We know that, too.

HENDERSON

But you're sending us to—

I 7

STARKEY

Yeah! Today, we're gonna bomb Constantinople right off
the map.

BAILEY

Why don't we just bomb the map?

HENDERSON

Constantinople isn't on the map. There just ain't no such
place any more.

STARKEY

(With breezy good humor)
Henderson, *ours* not to reason why. It's *yours* but to do as
you're told . . . and die.

SINCLAIR

Yeah. And that's why all of *us* are already dead.

STARKEY

(Consulting the sheet on his clipboard)
No, that isn't correct.

HENDERSON

Yes, it is. We're doomed, aren't we? So we're dead.

FISHER

The problem is, I don't know if we're dead or not.

JOE

What's the problem? We're here, we're alive, and . . .
(Singing)
"We're in the army now."
(Speaking)
So what's the problem?

(To the surprise of the men, their discussion is interrupted by Ruth, who walks in suddenly from the side in the manner of a sleepwalker, her posture and expression deliberately exaggerated.

Ruth is an attractive girl in her thirties, dressed in the uniform of a Red Cross worker stationed at the base. In one of the hands outstretched before her, she carries a glass coffee-maker; in the other, she carries a porcelain mug. She is talking loudly, emulating extravagantly an actress playing the role of someone in a trance.

The men react to her entrance with sounds and gestures of good-natured dismay and irritation. Ruth plays her remarks to the men and pays no attention to their disrespectful comments)

RUTH

Dead . . . dead . . . dead!

HENDERSON

Oh, Jesus! Look who's here.

RUTH

I want to speak. I want to feel. I want to touch.

BAILEY

Our angel of mercy!

RUTH

Why can't they hear me when I speak?

HENDERSON

Oh, get her out of here—someone?

RUTH

Why can't they feel me when I touch? I've been so much a part of them.

FISHER

Your mother and I have been very deeply concerned about you.

(Ruth turns suddenly from the men, drops her pose of high, romantic melodrama, and speaks to Starkey complainingly in an abrupt change to realism)

RUTH

If we were doing something beautiful here, I could say beautiful things like that. Instead, I've got to carry this stinking coffeepot back and forth. I don't want to carry a stinking coffeepot.

(Resumes her trancelike state as she moves to the Major and sets the mug of coffee on his desk)

I want to carry messages from the life ahead to generations of the life to come. I want to deliver poetic tidings of love and tenderness and call out—

(Retreats as the Major glares at her, and then moves forward to the footlights and speaks directly to the audience)

—call out to *all* of you, "Welcome, folks. Glad to have you all aboard with me on the ship of life." I want to make an everlasting imprint on the sands of time.

(Whining sourly)

I don't want to make stinking coffee and donuts.

MAJOR

Ruth?

RUTH

(Turning to him hopefully)
Yes?

MAJOR

Get the hell out of here!

(The Major jerks his thumb toward the wings. The men laugh and applaud and jeer)

JOE

(Singing)
"Good night, ladies."

HENDERSON

Give her the hook, the hook, the hook.

JOE

"Good night, ladies. Good night, ladies."

ALL

"We hate to see you go!"

(As the men hoot and roar with laughter, Ruth sticks her tongue out at them, makes an impatient face at the audience, thumbs her nose, first at the Major, then at the men, and hurries offstage, wiggling her backside deliberately)

HENDERSON

Glory be, Captain! Where did *we* get *her*?
(Looks meaningfully at Starkey)
As if I didn't know.

STARKEY

(A bit sheepishly)
Well, she is the second prettiest girl on the base.

JOE

She makes stinking coffee.

BAILEY

She's got a stinking coffeepot, that's why.

(Fisher moves forward toward Starkey)

FISHER

Captain Starkey?
    (Henderson makes the kissing noise again. Fisher
    casts him another look of annoyance before he re-
    sumes speaking to Starkey)
Sir? Are we really going to bomb Constantinople today?

STARKEY

Indeed we are, son.

FISHER

Is it very dangerous?

STARKEY

Yes, son. I'm afraid it is.

FISHER

Is anybody going to be killed?

STARKEY

Yeah.

FISHER

Who?

(Starkey stares at him without replying)

MAJOR
(His voice booming out)
Starkey!

STARKEY
Sir?

MAJOR
Come here now, please.

STARKEY
Yes, sir.

(Starkey turns and strides away toward the **Major**. Fisher calls after him)

FISHER
Who?
(Starkey does not reply. Fisher is left gaping after him, waiting in vain for an answer to his question. He turns after another second or two and moves back toward the others awkwardly, as though uncertain what to say or do next)
What do we do now?

JOE
We wait, kid. That's what we do.

(There is a gloomy, worried lull in which they all begin to shift in their seats or drift about restlessly)

HENDERSON
Why don't we sing a song now? Yeah, that's what *I* would do . . . if *I* was in charge.

23

BAILEY

Sure. We could try that. And I think I know just the song
we could—

JOE

(Opening his mouth wide suddenly and singing)
"Beeeeee . . ."

(Henderson, then Fisher, then—after a moment of
pique at being interrupted—Bailey, all join in on
that first note, and the words that follow are sung
to the tune of John Philip Sousa's "Stars and
Stripes Forever")

ALL FOUR

"Beeeeeee . . . kind to your web-footed friends.
For a duck may be somebody's mother.
They live in a stream by a swamp,
Where the weather is always damp."

(Sinclair sits in scowling silence. The others
cluster around him, trying to cheer him up and
urging him unsuccessfully to join in)

SINCLAIR

Aw, cut it out, for Christ sakes!
(Sinclair springs up and shoves his way through
them)
Cut it out!
(They break off singing)
What the hell are you all singing about? We've got this
goddam mission to fly. Constantinople—gee whiz!

BAILEY

So . . . we won't sing a song.

FISHER

(To Sinclair)
It's okay. I'm scared of this mission today too.

SINCLAIR

You? What are *you* scared about? I'm the one that has to
be killed.

JOE

I'm a little scared also. I'm starting to get a little scared of
all of them.

HENDERSON

I'm not.

BAILEY

Aren't you worried at all?

HENDERSON

Nah, not me. And should I tell you why?

(The others press close with curiosity)

FISHER

Why?

HENDERSON

Because I'm not really a soldier, that's why. I'm really
something much different. I'm an *actor* . . . playing the
part of a soldier.

(Indicating the audience)
They know that.

(Smiling, he addresses the audience directly)
Right? And I'm pretty good, too.

25

(To Sinclair)
It's just a little game we're having here now. It's only a play, a show, a little entertainment, so let's not get carried away too far and forget who we *really* are.

SINCLAIR
Yeah, sure.

HENDERSON
Sinclair—this soldier I'm pretending to be never even lived, so how could I get killed? He's fictitious, a figment of somebody's imagination. I never met him, and I don't care about him. So what do I give a damn how many guns they've got at Constantinople or what that dumb slob of a Major says. Huh?

BAILEY
So? How come you keep complaining all the time?

HENDERSON
Because my part is too small, that's why.
   (To the audience)
I'm really the most important one here. And I'll tell you all something else. I'm also the best one. Did any of you people see me last year in _____?
   (Names the best-known play or movie he was actually in recently. He turns to address the other men on stage)
Did any of *you* see me in _____?

BAILEY
I did.
   (Pauses, while Henderson waits expectantly)
You stank.

HENDERSON

You're jealous, Bailey. You want to be the sergeant here, don't you, even though you wouldn't know how to handle it.

> (Disconsolately, almost without realizing what he is doing, he takes hold of a piece of the wall and shakes it, providing a visible, unconscious reminder that it is only stage scenery)

Aaah, what do any of us know about what's really going on here?

SINCLAIR

I put in ———.

> (He supplies a true fact from his actual experience as an actor)

HENDERSON

A lot that will get you.

SINCLAIR

It got me a part in here.

HENDERSON

Some part. You'll be gone before anyone knows you're even here.

> (To the others as well)

Hey, you know who's really killing things? Our famous Captain Starkey. I should be the captain.

FISHER

You're too young to be a captain.

JOE

I'm the oldest one here, and I'm only a Pfc.

HENDERSON

What does age mean? I could do everything in this war.
He can't do anything.

FISHER

It's a hard role to play. He doesn't know whether he's on
our side or theirs.

JOE

He's on their side. He's an officer, ain't he? And all he does
is what the Major tells him. That's all he's supposed to do.

FISHER

That's what I mean. He's got nothing to hang on to. He's
got no point of view of his own. That's a very difficult part
to play.

HENDERSON

Not for me. I'd turn him into a hero. I'd put fire into his
lines.
    (Imitating Starkey)
None of this "Greetings. You are all hereby ordered . . .
to a war." I'd give you . . . volume. I'd give you . . .
    (Strides proudly forward and recites to the audi-
    ence)
"Once more unto the breach, dear friends, once more;
Or close the wall up with our English dead."
    (Speaking normally)
Oh boy! I'd stir the whole joint up. I'd give you . . .
    (Calling out into the theater at the top of his voice)
"Cry God for Harry! England and Saint George!"
    (To the men, speaking normally)
Well? How's that?

BAILEY

You still stink.

FISHER

Yeah. And this isn't Henry the Fifth either. I don't know *what* it is, because I'm not sure what's going on.

JOE

It's a war, kid, that's what's going on. We're in a big, dangerous war, kid, so what's the problem?

FISHER

Okay, then it's a war. But what are we doing here? Who are we fighting, and who are we really supposed to be? I mean—are we really flying a mission to Constantinople today, or are we just making believe?

SINCLAIR

That's right. If we are going, *why* are we going? What's our motivation?

HENDERSON

Our motivation? Oh, I know our motivation.

SINCLAIR

Then tell us. What's making us go?

HENDERSON

(As the others press close)
The Major! *That's* our motivation. *That's* what's making us go . . . that old hippopotamus of a—

(The men laugh and begin kidding around noisily with each other)

MAJOR

(To Starkey)
Sergeant Henderson.

STARKEY

Sergeant Henderson!

(Henderson draws himself to attention)

HENDERSON

Sir?

STARKEY

Front, please!

HENDERSON

Yes, sir!

(As Henderson starts away toward the officers, Fisher is able to give back to him the contemptuous kissing noise)

FISHER

Go get 'em, tiger. Ha, ha!

(The men resume their boisterous horseplay as Henderson walks across stage to the officers. They sing a fragment of the Sousa march and then begin mocking Henderson's recitation from *Henry V*)

HENDERSON

(To the Major)
Sir?

MAJOR

Keep those men quiet. You're supposed to be in charge now.

HENDERSON

Yes, sir!

(To the men as he returns to them, loudly and officiously, for the Major's benefit)

Okay, you guys, keep it down, keep it down. Hear?

MAJOR

Bring them in now and let's go on.

STARKEY

All right, men. It's time to go to work. Move along. Let's go.

(At Starkey's loud and peremptory tone, the men snap back into attitudes of military obedience and hurry across stage into the area of the Major's office. They start to line up at attention there in two rows, the idiots all in the rear one. Starkey moves forward to speed them along)

Hurry up, boys. It's time.

HENDERSON

(Correcting him derisively)

Hurry up, *please* . . .

STARKEY

(Grimacing angrily)

Hurry up, *please* . . .

FISHER

(Furtively, the last to follow)

. . . it's time.

(Starkey jerks around and reacts with another grimace to Fisher's gibe. The Major waits until the

men are all lined up in their two rows and then
moves around in front of his desk to address them)

MAJOR

Okay, men, you all know where you are going now and
what we're supposed to do. Is everything absolutely clear?

HENDERSON

Are we really going to bomb Constantinople?

MAJOR

Yes.

HENDERSON

Why?

MAJOR

(Reflects a moment and decides to answer)
This mission to Constantinople today is a military man's
dream. It's a sneak attack. Are there any other questions?

BAILEY

Why are we killing Turks?

MAJOR

That's none of our business. Are there any other questions?
(The men remain silent)
This is a good mission you people are flying today. If
everything goes well, there shouldn't be a single thing in
Constantinople left alive. This is a mission we can all be
very proud of.

SINCLAIR

I don't like it. I don't like it at all.

MAJOR

Why not?

SINCLAIR

It should come at the end of the last act, that's why. I don't want to be killed so early.

(The men laugh)

Yeah, it's easy for all of *you* to laugh. But I'm the one that's going to be killed now. And I've only just got here.

(To the Major)

Why can't I get killed in the last act?

MAJOR

Somebody else gets killed in the last act.

SINCLAIR

Why can't I get killed then?

MAJOR

Because you get killed now.

SINCLAIR

I don't want to die so soon. I don't even want to be here any more.

MAJOR

You should have thought of that before you volunteered.

SINCLAIR

I didn't volunteer.

MAJOR

That doesn't matter. You *are* here, and there isn't a single thing you can do about it now. Stand up at attention the

33

way you're supposed to and show some respect for my
position.

(Sinclair hesitates, then yields and stands up at
attention)

Now get back in line.

(Sinclair steps back in line, where the others are
standing in relaxed positions, watching and murmuring with amusement)

All of you! From now on, all of you stand up at attention
whenever I talk to you.

(The men come to attention immediately, all but
Henderson, who deliberates a moment and then
strolls forward out of line and stands waiting before the Major in insolent defiance. The Major
studies him a moment)

All right. What's the matter with you?

HENDERSON

(Points toward the globe)

I'd like to blow up the whole fucking thing.

(Everyone on stage starts with vivid surprise—
even the Major—and all turn to stare at Henderson with amazement. Starkey, as though he has
finally had all he can take, moves belligerently to
the globe)

STARKEY

(Pointing to the globe)

Do you mean this?

HENDERSON

Yes, I mean that. That's what I would do if I were in
charge, instead of picking it apart so slowly, piece by

piece and person by person by person. Why don't we just smash the whole fucking thing to bits once and for all and get it over with?

STARKEY

Is that right? You want to smash the whole thing to bits right now?

HENDERSON

Yeah.

(Starkey and Henderson glare at each other. Starkey glances toward the Major. The Major nods, giving a signal of approval. Starkey turns back to Henderson)

STARKEY

(Taunting)
Okay. Go ahead.
(Then, to Henderson's surprise, Starkey lifts the globe out of the stand and tosses it to Henderson, who reaches out instinctively to catch it)
Smash it. Go on. Smash it to bits.

HENDERSON

Can I? Can I really?

STARKEY

Sure. Go ahead. Smash it. And after you've done it . . . what will you have?

(Henderson hesitates a moment, on the verge of hurling the globe to the floor, then relaxes suddenly and smiles)

35

HENDERSON

Bits.

(Henderson, yielding, tosses the globe back to Starkey)

STARKEY

That's right, Henderson. Bits.

(Starkey replaces the globe in the stand)

MAJOR

(To Henderson)
Are you ready to continue now?

HENDERSON

Yeah. Sure.

MAJOR

Then say *sir* when you talk to me!

HENDERSON

(Snapping to attention)
Yes, sir!

MAJOR

And get back in line with the rest of them.

HENDERSON

Yes, sir!

(Henderson responds obediently and takes his place in the line with the rest. Sinclair suddenly takes an impulsive step forward)

SINCLAIR

What about me? Shouldn't I raise a bigger stink now about getting killed?

MAJOR

No. Get back in line where you belong.
(Sinclair hesitates a second, as though tempted to rebel, and then steps back into line, resentful for a moment, and then cooperative. The Major is satisfied)
That's better. Yes, you're all doing fine now. Let's get this mission to Constantinople over with as quickly as we can. You're all due back here in exactly eighteen minutes for calisthenics. Any more questions?

FISHER

Sir?
(The Major turns to him)
Can I bring my kid brother?

MAJOR

Not yet. Any other? Then get going.
(As the men fall out of line)
And take all this junk with you.
(By junk, he means the stage scenery, and the men divide up into carefully drilled groups to begin clearing the stage. Henderson exits with one of the props. The area containing the Major and Starkey is saved for last. The Major takes up his manuscript and prepares to leave)
I'm not sure about Henderson.

STARKEY

I don't like him. He's a conceited, disobedient, unreliable little punk.

(The Major erases Sinclair's name from the list on
the blackboard)

MAJOR

I'm glad you feel that way. I'm getting rid of him soon.

STARKEY

I think that's good. Major?

MAJOR

Yes?

STARKEY

Who gets killed in the last act?

MAJOR

You'll never guess.

STARKEY

Me?

MAJOR

No, of course not. You're safe, Starkey. Trust me. You'll
always be safe, because you do your job and you don't take
chances. So relax and take it easy, have fun, marry your
girl friend. Nothing bad ever happens to you.

STARKEY

Major? One more question. What's it all about?

MAJOR

(Encompassing the script, the stage, the theater,
and the audience in a single, sweeping gesture)
This? It's about time.

STARKEY

No, it isn't. It's about war.

MAJOR

(Motioning toward the clock)
You'll find out.

(The Major departs with a wave, carrying his
script. Starkey begins collecting his clipboard,
his newspaper, and his portfolio as Sinclair and a
few of the other men march across stage to push the
office area in which he is standing out of sight into
the wing. Starkey exits with it.

With the briefing room gone, the stage affords a
broad, empty area that is bright, deep, and inde-
finable, a little weird and a little mysterious. There
is room enough now for the characters, even when
all together, to cavort in freely; at the same time
there is a feeling of sterility and desolation that
arises from the very bareness and spaciousness,
and every now and then one or another of them
will roam about the limits moodily, as though
probing in a void. Most of the activities that take
place while the stage is bare will be remindful of
the sunny outdoors. Yet, there is always the sense,
however faint, that the space is really very firmly
enclosed, and that the people inside it are enclosed
with it. There will be occasional troubled lulls
when the enlisted men are on the bare stage, as
though they are not sure what to do next.

When the last element of the briefing room has
been removed, the stage remains empty and totally
silent for several seconds.

When someone does appear, finally, it turns out

to be Ruth, who enters slowly, wheeling in a rattling coffee wagon of a kind commonly seen in office buildings. Plain brown donuts are stacked on upright wooden sticks. There are drinking mugs on the wagon near the coffee urn.

Ruth stops and looks around uncertainly. She seems surprised to find herself alone; she fidgets uncomfortably, straightens her skirt. She peers offstage in different directions from which other people might enter. She looks at her watch, waits another second or two, shrugs, and begins talking. At first, she seems to be ruminating aloud; but after her first few phrases, it becomes obvious that she is addressing the audience directly)

RUTH

If I were a dumb broad . . . or a vulgar person . . . I would say something stupid now . . . or something dirty like . . . like—uh . . . *son-of-a-bitch* . . . and most of you would probably laugh. But, I'm not a dumb broad . . . or a vulgar person . . . so I won't say something stupid . . . or *son-of-a-bitch* . . . and none of you will laugh.

(Starkey returns while she speaks, carrying his newspaper and his portfolio. His own comment will be determined by whether or not the audience has laughed)

STARKEY

Ruthie, you are (aren't) a dumb broad, you did (didn't) say something stupid, and that's why they did (didn't) laugh.

(Takes a donut and reaches for an empty cup)
Gimme some coffee, will you? Maybe it will stimulate me for what happens next.

RUTH

What happens next?

STARKEY

I have to interrogate. I have to take all the men off someplace where nobody can see me and ask them some very important questions I'm not interested in.

RUTH

When?

STARKEY

In a couple of minutes. We just got through with that mission to Constantinople.

RUTH

Oh, really? How did it go?

STARKEY

I'll let you know when I interrogate. Say, Ruthie girl. What are you doing when you're finished here?

RUTH

I might be busy.

STARKEY

Don't be. I think I might want a hunk.

RUTH

(Indignant)
A hunk of what?

STARKEY

A hunk of you.

RUTH

Now isn't that too bad? You know, Starkey, just about the only time you want to see me is when *you* want to see me.

STARKEY

It's my unselfish nature. I do that only for *your* own good. I would be pretty bad company if I began hanging around you when I *didn't* want to see you.

RUTH

And what am I supposed to do in between? Grind coffee beans? Or should I start giving *hunks* away to somebody else?

STARKEY

(Teasing her)
Oh, that reminds me, honey. Are you sort of—er—sleeping with Henderson?

RUTH

I'm sort of—er—not sure. Which one is he?

STARKEY

The sergeant.

RUTH

Not yet.

STARKEY

Are you sleeping with the Major?

RUTH

Not any more.

STARKEY

Oh, come on, Ruthie. Give me a straight answer. I'm
jealous.

RUTH

(Skeptical)
Really?

STARKEY

Maybe.

RUTH

Then you give me one. Are *you* married?

(Starkey gasps with surprise and spews out coffee)

STARKEY

Jesus Christ, Ruthie! Where's your manners? That's a
helluva goddam personal question to ask a gentleman
you *are* sleeping with!

RUTH

Then let's try another. Do you love me?

STARKEY

That's even worse!

RUTH

Well, I've got to know, dammit! I don't know who I am
here or what I mean to anybody. I don't know how I'm
supposed to act with you or anybody else. Am I just a
goddam Red Cross girl? Is that all I mean to you? If you
get killed—

43

STARKEY

I don't get killed.

RUTH

If you did get killed, am I heartbroken?

STARKEY

I would expect the whole world to be heartbroken.

RUTH

Starkey, stop smiling *all* the time. Please? There's not that much to smile about.

STARKEY

Okay. What's bothering you?

RUTH

I don't know how to respond to you. I don't know what I'm supposed to say to you . . . or even how I ought to feel about you. That's why I have to know. Do you love me, or don't you?

STARKEY

Okay, I'll tell you. Do you want the truth, or do you want a lie?

RUTH

Which is better?

STARKEY

I'd go with the lie if I were you.

RUTH

No. I want the truth. Do you love me?

44

STARKEY

No.

RUTH

Let's have the lie.

STARKEY

Yes, I do love you, Ruth, more than I could ever say.

RUTH

Darling!
(Ruth flings herself dramatically into Starkey's arms, and the two embrace passionately with an ardor that is definitely histrionic)

STARKEY

And, my darling, do you know what I love best about you?

RUTH

My body?

STARKEY

Right.
(Ruth pulls away from him with a smile and begins strutting proudly)

RUTH

It is a great body, isn't it? The head's a little worn. But the thighs are good, and the boobs are still first-rate.

STARKEY

You're the second prettiest girl on the base.

45

RUTH

I used to be the first prettiest. Then they sent another girl
here. How do you like my coffee today?
 (Starkey gives her a long, meaningful look)
I know—it stinks, doesn't it? So what? I'm an actress, not
a cook. I can play anything.

STARKEY

Except a cook.

RUTH

What kind of part is a cook? I could play Victoria Regina.
I could play——————.
 (She mentions the name of any very popular and
 glamorous movie actress and attempts an imitation)
I can play Liza Doolittle, the cockney, or I can even play
Cordelia in *King Lear* by William Shakespeare of Eng-
land.

STARKEY

The hell you could!

RUTH

I could.

STARKEY

You couldn't keep your mouth shut long enough to play
Cordelia. When Lear turns to you finally and says:
 (Reciting)
                    "Now, our joy,
Although our last, not least; to whose young love
The vines of France and milk of Burgundy
Strive to be interess'd; what can you say to draw
A third more opulent than your sisters? Speak."

46

RUTH

Hey, that's good. And what do I say?

STARKEY

"Nothing."

RUTH

Nothing?

STARKEY

That's right, "Nothing."

RUTH

Oh.
(Drawing the word out into a large, dramatic
moment)
"Nothing."

STARKEY

Yeah. And that's just where *you'd* get into trouble, when
all you had to say was: "Nothing." You would drop dead
from frustration right there on the stage!

RUTH

I would not!

STARKEY

No, of course not! You'd start gushing compliments all
over the foolish old king and ruin the next four acts!
(Starkey and Ruth are both laughing now, and
they embrace again, more naturally and more
earnestly than before)
Honey, you *are* cute . . . and crazy. Better pour some

47

more coffee. I think I hear my idiots now, all marching
back proudly from *Constantinople*.

(As Ruth begins pouring coffee into a line of cups,
there is heard from offstage the sound of a voice
counting marching cadence. Starkey takes over the
cadence count as the first of the men enter)

Hup, two, three, four! Hup, two, three, four! That's the
way, to earn your pay! Hup, two, three, four!

(The five Idiots enter first; Bailey, Joe, and Fisher
follow. Only the Idiots march to the cadence count.
The others straggle, looking tired and bored, and
head straight for the coffee wagon. The Idiots continue marching across stage and exit)

RUTH

Come and get it, boys. Hot coffee. Fresh donuts.

(Bailey, Joe, and Fisher pick up cups and sip.
They react instantly to the vile taste of the coffee.
They put the cups down, glare at Ruth indignantly,
and move offstage, staring back at her with resentment mixed with incredulity.

Starkey waits until they have all gone, then prepares to follow)

STARKEY

Stick around, baby. I'll be back to claim you as soon as
I'm through.

RUTH

I might not be here.

STARKEY

Oh, you'll be here.

48

RUTH

Is that so? And just what makes you so sure?

(Starkey laughs confidently and points—to the
Major, who comes onstage then carrying his manuscript. Starkey leaves, thumbing his nose at Ruth.
The Major looks rather pleased with things as
he heads for the coffee wagon. His relaxed and
amiable manner suggests that he is taking a break.
Ruth pours a cup of coffee for him, then preens herself a bit)

MAJOR

Let's have a donut please, Ruth. Two.

RUTH

Sure. How is it going?

MAJOR

Pretty good, I would say. We got through that mission to
Constantinople without too much trouble, didn't we? And
that was the hardest part.

RUTH

Is there anything *I* can do? I've got lots of ability.

(The Major bites into the donut and is startled by
what he tastes)

MAJOR

Make better donuts. Where's Henderson? *Henderson!*
(The Major is irritated and reverts to his former
manner of brusque authority)
He should be coming on and walking through here right
now. *Henderson!*

49

(After another few seconds, Henderson enters, walking wearily and despondently, his head down. He seems unaware of the Major or Ruth and moves as though he has not come on in response to the Major's call. His clothes are covered with matted blood. He walks as though in a daze, acting—and acting very well—the role of a soldier exhausted by combat.

Henderson does not head for the coffee wagon but moves directly across stage. The Major watches him with an angry frown for a few moments; then the Major falls into a role of his own and begins walking across stage in a direction that brings him toward Henderson. Only when they are almost abreast of each other does Henderson appear to see him. He straightens immediately and salutes. The Major returns the salute, and they both stop. Both are playing roles now—but playing them very seriously)

MAJOR

Rough over Constantinople, wasn't it?

HENDERSON

Yes, sir. It was . . . rough.

MAJOR

I know. And I'm sorry. I'm proud of you today, Henderson. Very proud.

HENDERSON

Thank you, sir. And God bless you.
(They exchange salutes again as the Major resumes walking and exits. Henderson walks a few

steps and then takes a furtive peek over his
shoulder. When he sees that the Major has gone,
his whole manner changes instantly, as though he
is dropping out of the role he has been performing
once there is nobody to supervise him. He stops,
lets out an exclamation of condescending contempt,
and saunters casually toward the coffee wagon)
Oh, boy—what I have to go through! I'm glad you're
here. Gimme some coffee, sweetie, will you? I'm beat.

RUTH

(Pours a cup)
Say please.

HENDERSON

Drop dead.

RUTH

I love *you*, too.

HENDERSON

I don't blame you.

RUTH

How do you like my coffee?

HENDERSON

It really stinks.

(Henderson moves to the sugar bowl and keeps
dropping spoonful after spoonful of sugar into his
cup as they continue talking)

RUTH

How do you like me?

51

HENDERSON

Quiet.

RUTH

You know who's jealous of you?

HENDERSON

Everybody.

RUTH

Captain Starkey.

HENDERSON

He's got a right to be. He stinks too.

RUTH

Did you tell him you were sleeping with me?

HENDERSON

Why would I do that?

RUTH

He thinks you are.

HENDERSON

He's crazy.

RUTH

What's so crazy about it? I could be your mistress.

HENDERSON

You're too old. You could be my mother.

RUTH

I could play Juliet to your Romeo—if *you* could play a Romeo. Say, I've got a hot idea.
(Suggestively)
Let's play *Oedipus Rex* together.

HENDERSON

Jesus—you've got a filthy mind!

RUTH

I've got talent, that's what I've got. But they won't let me use it. I don't even have any good lines. I've got to *make* them funny if I want to make people laugh.

HENDERSON

You're not supposed to make people laugh. You're supposed to make people coffee.

RUTH

See? *You* get that line, not me. Hey, what's that stuff you've got all over you?

HENDERSON

(With scarcely any concern)
This? It's blood.

RUTH

You've got an awful lot there.

HENDERSON

I used all he had.

RUTH

Where'd you get it?

53

HENDERSON

From Sinclair.

RUTH

Which one is he?

HENDERSON

He's that kid who ——————.
(Inserts fact used earlier from Sinclair's previous acting experience)
He was killed just now on the mission to Constantinople.

RUTH

Really?

HENDERSON

Yeah. He died in my arms just a little while ago. Hey, what's the matter with you?

(Ruth is distraught and virtually in tears)

RUTH

Oh, that's terrible! He's really dead? I get so broken up when I hear something like that. Oh, that poor, poor little kid!

HENDERSON

Okay. You don't have to make such a big scene out of it.

RUTH

No? How am I supposed to act? Brave? No, thanks! That's one part I *don't* want!

HENDERSON

He wasn't really killed, you know. He isn't really dead.

RUTH

Where is he, then? Show him to me.

HENDERSON

Okay, I'll show him to you.
(Bailey, Joe, and Fisher enter and move across
stage)
Hey, Bailey . . . Joe! Sinclair? Is he out over there?

BAILEY

No. Of course not.

JOE

(To Bailey, puzzled by Henderson's question)
Sinclair?

(Bailey, Joe, and Fisher exit. Henderson starts
away, speaking to Ruth as he goes)

HENDERSON

You just wait here. I'll get him.

RUTH

Okay. Get him.

HENDERSON

I'll get him. I'll bring him right back here.

RUTH

Go ahead—get him.

(Henderson exits with annoyance, leaving Ruth
alone onstage. Ruth gazes after him with a look of
intense grief)

RUTH

(Softly at first)

Oh, God! God . . . God . . . God!

(Ruth turns and drifts forward. She speaks directly
to the audience with a deep sincerity of emotion)

Another young boy killed in a war. And all of you just
sat there. It happened right now. Didn't you care? Doesn't
it mean anything to you?

(Starkey strolls in while Ruth is speaking and
halts, as though taken aback to see her so deeply
moved. He carries his newspaper and his business-
man's portfolio)

STARKEY

Hey, Ruthie! *Ruthie!* Take it easy, will you? What do
you want from *them?* This is only a play. They never heard
of this character Sinclair before. He's a stranger to them.
He's like a name in this newspaper.

RUTH

(To Starkey)

What difference does *that* make? He's dead, isn't he?

(Throws her hands up disgustedly)

Aaaah, what do I care? I don't even know anybody
in _____.

(Names the city in which the play is being performed. She moves to the coffee wagon and pours a
cup of coffee for herself, addressing the audience,
rather than Starkey, as she continues)

Why should I be the one to worry and cry over other
people, when nobody else does? I can cry over myself—
God knows I've got enough to cry about, and God knows

I want to cry often enough. I'm a girl, and I'm thirty-four years old.

(She makes a face, realizing what she has just said)

He thinks I'm only thirty. Don't you?

(Looks at Starkey, who shrugs and shakes his head noncommittally)

I've never been married, and if I had been, I'd probably be divorced. My face isn't too good, and my skin isn't so soft any more, in spite of all those rejuvenating facial oils I've been packing on. And, if the truth must be told, my body is not quite as good as it may look; it's kind of—er—propped up a little here and there. All in all, I have to admit I'm getting a little long in the tooth. I never really knew what I wanted to be—except a pretty girl, a happy sweetheart, a blushing bride, and a good wife. And a wonderful mother. Oh, what a wonderful mother I used to think I would make! Since it didn't look like I could become any of those, I had a crack at acting. For a while I wanted to be a nurse . . . but I couldn't type. For the time being, I'm a Red Cross worker—

(Sips the coffee and reacts to its bad taste)

—and I can't make coffee. I don't want to sound conceited, but I think I would be an awfully good thing for somebody who wanted me. But nobody wants me, not for very long.

STARKEY

I want you.

RUTH

For very long?

57

(Starkey shrugs evasively again, murmuring something almost inaudibly)

STARKEY

Well . . . I mean . . . nobody . . .

(Ruth turns from him to address the audience again)

RUTH

So tell me, all you safe and distinguished and successful people, who sit there so amiably while I grow old and pour my heart out, and while a nice young man who never did you any harm is ordered to fly to Constantinople and be killed—what do I do now?

STARKEY

Let's go to bed.

RUTH

And what do I say to that?

(The Major enters, carrying his manuscript. He is accompanied by the Golfer and the Hunter, two gentlemen of middle age who are dressed in a way appropriate to their respective hobbies. Both these Sportsmen radiate an affluence and geniality that are suggestive of middle-class business executives out on a harmless spree. They grin, as though with delight to find themselves on a stage in a crowded theater, and stare about with happy shyness and uncertainty. The Golfer carries a golf club; the Hunter carries a shotgun. The Major speaks to Ruth as though prompting her, supplying the answer to her question)

MAJOR

Say yes.

RUTH

(Makes a face at the Major and then says, soul-
fully, to Starkey)
Ye-e-e-e-s.

(In trite, theatrical tradition, Ruth and Starkey
fall into each other's arms)

GOLFER

Who is she?

MAJOR

She's our Red Cross girl.

(The Golfer winks knowingly and chortles in
lascivious expectation)

RUTH

Starkey, it's really important, so tell me the truth. Please.
Are you married or aren't you?

STARKEY

Just *why* is that so important?

RUTH

I'm going to have a baby.

(Starkey gawks and lets out a low whistle of surprise)

STARKEY

And what do *I* say to *that?*

RUTH

You might ask me if it's yours.

STARKEY

We know it's *yours*. Is it mine?

RUTH

Do you want the truth, or do you want a lie?

STARKEY

Which is better?

RUTH

It's yours.

STARKEY

(Yielding)
I'm not married.

RUTH

Will you? Will you marry me now?

(Starkey looks over her shoulder at the Major.
The Major nods, giving permission)

STARKEY

Sure.
(They embrace tenderly)
Can I smile a little now?

RUTH

Yes.

STARKEY

Can I sing?

RUTH

No.

(He does anyway)

STARKEY

"Just Molly and me."

RUTH

"And baby makes three."

BOTH

"We're happy in our blue heaven."

(Together, while singing, they take the handle of
the coffee wagon and wheel it offstage as though it
were a baby carriage. The Major watches them go
with an approving smile)

MAJOR

It's going pretty well, I'd say. Right?

GOLFER

I love it.

HUNTER

I think it's great. I'm proud to be one of the backers.

MAJOR

That's fine, then. Now this is the stage—that's all there is
to it. This is the proscenium, up there are the flies, and out
there in the theater is the audience.

GOLFER

How many seats are there?

MAJOR

Here? —————.

(He gives the exact number of seats in the theater
in which the play is being performed)

It's a small (big) theater, but it's a good place for us to
work from now.

GOLFER

Suppose we bomb here?

HUNTER

Yeah. Suppose they don't like us?

MAJOR

I'll blast them off the map.

HUNTER

You mean that?

MAJOR

Why not? We just killed them in Constantinople, didn't
we? I can kill these people here just as well.

GOLFER

I think that's marvelous. What happens next?

MAJOR

We bomb in Minnesota.

HUNTER

That sounds like fun. Right now?

MAJOR

Oh, no, a little later. First Henderson brings the men out
for some exercise. Then I have Starkey come out with
some new war equipment that will really stop the show.

GOLFER

That captain's pretty good, isn't he?

MAJOR

He's all right.

HUNTER

(Surprised)
Don't you like him?

MAJOR

(Without emotion)
No.

HUNTER

Why don't you get rid of him?

MAJOR

I won't have to. He does everything I want him to do, and
he does it very well. Wait till you see how beautifully he
handles Henderson, and what he does with all that new
equipment he brings out.

GOLFER

I can *hardly* wait.

HUNTER

Me neither.
    (He lights a cigar)
Say, why don't you let the men smoke?

MAJOR

Because they want to.

GOLFER

That sounds funny too. Listen, I'd like to have a part in this, sort of. Could you kind of—er—arrange that?

MAJOR

Are you sure you want to?

GOLFER

And how!

HUNTER

Me too. I've never really been in one before.

MAJOR

Okay, both of you. Keep your gun and your club. I'll get you some uniforms.
    (Looks at his watch)
Stand together there now, and I'll teach you a few things. Good. Now . . . 'tention!
        (Grinning with delight to find themselves playing soldier, the Golfer and the Hunter snap clumsily to attention; they are not quite sure what to do with the golf club and the shotgun. The Major watches them pleasantly)
Present . . . arms!
        (The Sportsmen are at a complete loss. Using his manuscript as a weapon, the Major counts them through the stages of what they are intended to do. On the second attempt they get it right, and the three go through the maneuver together, one using a golf club, one a shotgun, and the Major his script)
Shoulder . . . arms!

(Again, the Major uses his script to demonstrate,
and the Sportsmen learn quickly)
Very good. You've got a natural aptitude for this.
(Looks toward the wing impatiently and waits a
few seconds more before speaking)
And now, where the hell is Henderson? *Henderson!* He's
always late. He's supposed to be bringing those men out
here for calisthenics right now!

HUNTER

Why don't you get rid of him?

MAJOR

I'm going to, very soon. *Henderson!* I'm going to kill him
on that mission to Minnesota. *Henderson!*
(From offstage, in the distance, there suddenly
sounds the voice of someone counting out double-
time cadence. Gradually, together with the noise of
running feet pounding in step, the voice draws
closer)
Here he comes. Okay . . . let's go. Forward . . . *march!*
Left, right, left, right, that's good, left, right.
(Smirking self-consciously, the Sportsmen begin
marching away awkwardly in the same direction
from which the men are coming. The first of the
men appear, jogging on stage in single file. They
are dressed in sweatshirts and athletic shorts, and
they wear sneakers. The first in line are the five
Idiots; then come Fisher and Joe. The man in
charge is running alongside; when he enters, he
turns out to be not Henderson, but Bailey! The
Major is amazed and barks his first words at the
two Sportsmen)
Halt—hold it! Bailey! Bailey!

65

BAILEY

Yes, sir.

(Bailey pulls away from the line of trotting men
and stops at attention in front of the Major. Un-
noticed by either, the other men keep trotting across
stage and go out of sight on the other side)

MAJOR

Where's Henderson?

BAILEY

I don't know, sir. He wasn't there when you began calling,
so I thought I'd better bring the men out here. Did I do
right, sir?

MAJOR

I'll find him. You keep them busy until Captain Starkey
gets here.

BAILEY

Yes, sir. Okay, you men—
    (Bailey turns to issue an order and perceives with
    astonishment that the men have trotted out of sight.
    With alarm he starts after them, running offstage
    as he shouts at the top of his voice)
Hey, come back! Come back, men. About . . . face! To the
rear . . . run!
    (In response to the order the men reappear, trotting
    back onstage like expressionless automatons in re-
    verse order and almost trampling Bailey underfoot.
    Bailey untangles himself from them and turns to
    the Major to apologize)
I'm sorry, sir. I—

66

(Again with alarm, Bailey notices that the men are
about to trot out of sight now on the other side of
the stage)
Men! Group! Squadron! Army!

(He looks at the Major in total confusion)

MAJOR

Company!

BAILEY

(Running after them)
Hey, company—to the rear . . . run!
(The men trot back onstage again, heading in
their original direction in their original order)
Sir. I—men! Men!

(Bailey grows flustered with the realization that
the men are heading offstage away from him again.
The Major steps away from Bailey to take over
before they run completely from sight)

MAJOR

Company, halt!
(The men stop)
Right face! Parade rest! At ease!

BAILEY

I'm sorry, sir. I guess I'm not used to taking Henderson's
place—yet.

MAJOR

I can see that. Do you know what you're supposed to do
next?

BAILEY

I think so. Straddle jumps and pushups.

MAJOR

Then do it.
(To the Sportsmen)
We'll go. 'tention! Forward march. Hut, two, three, four, hut, two, three . . .

(The Major counts the Sportsmen off the stage, then stops to watch Bailey, who springs into action)

BAILEY

Okay, men. Straddle jumps. Hands high overhead when you clap them, legs wide apart when you jump. Touch the sky, touch the sky. One, two, three, four, one, two, three, four, one . . .
(The Major goes, and Bailey stops almost immediately, in mid-sentence)
. . . two, three—you lousy sons of bitches!
(The men break formation and sprawl out indolently, a few of them lighting cigarettes, while Bailey prowls about among them in resentful frustration)
Why'd you make me look so stupid in front of the Major?

JOE

You are stupid. You don't even know how to give good commands for close-order drill.

BAILEY

What a chance I had! What a golden opportunity! There we were, just me and the Major . . .

68

FISHER

And us.

BAILEY

Yeah . . . and *you*. How could you all be so dumb? Why'd you keep running back and forth like that? Where the hell did you think you were running to?

JOE

We were only doing what you told us to do?

BAILEY

Why'd you have to *listen* to me? Look—I could be a better sergeant than he is, if you guys would only pitch in next time and cooperate.

FISHER

You can stop crying now and relax. Here he comes.

JOE

And I'm only a Pfc.

(Henderson enters slowly from a direction opposite the one in which he left, moving as though in a perplexed and brooding daze. He looks behind him, nibbling his lip, and studies the people onstage. He is still wearing his blood-spattered combat uniform)

HENDERSON

Who's got a cigarette?
(He pulls a cigarette from Joe's mouth as he passes him and moves about restlessly in a kind of aimless search)
Thanks.

69

JOE

Hey!

BAILEY

Where the hell have you been?

(Bailey's question does not register on Henderson
for three or four seconds. Henderson stops with
surprise when it does)

HENDERSON

What did you just say?

BAILEY

I said where the hell have you been?

HENDERSON

What the hell is that your business?

BAILEY

You're supposed to bring these men the hell out here. Not
me. The Major was looking for you.

HENDERSON

The hell with him, too. Where the hell is Sinclair?

(The others exchange a puzzled look)

JOE

Who?

(Henderson meditates gloomily a moment and then
comes forward to take the others into his confidence)

HENDERSON

Listen. I've been looking for Sinclair. I can't find him.

BAILEY

He's dead.

FISHER

He was just killed on the mission to Constantinople.

BAILEY

Maybe that's why you can't find him.

HENDERSON

I know all that. But where is he really? Right now.

BAILEY

In Heaven?

JOE

In Hell.

BAILEY

I'll betcha nickel.

(Henderson pulls away from them angrily, re-
buffed by their unwillingness to take him seriously)

HENDERSON

Stop clowning, will you? I've looked all over for him.
(With a gesture of his arm he takes in the entire
stage and the backstage area)
I can't find him.

BAILEY

Did you look in the toilet?

FISHER

Maybe he's in the hospital.

7 1

BAILEY

Or in the morgue.

JOE

He's dead, that's where he is. Maybe he's in the cemetery already. That's where dead people are.

HENDERSON

Oh, you idiots!

JOE

   (Pointing)
They're the idiots. Not us.

HENDERSON

Christ—you guys are kidding, aren't you? You don't think Sinclair was really killed, do you? You don't think he's really dead, do—
   (From offstage, there comes all at once the clear
   sound of a bugle playing Taps. For a few seconds,
   the men are all stricken with surprise. Then, as the
   melancholy music continues, Bailey, Joe, and
   Fisher burst out together into raucous laughter,
   taunting Henderson, who whirls away in furious
   disgust)
Oh, Jesus Christ! How corny can you get!

BAILEY

We were right! Bigshot, hotshot, wiseguy!

FISHER

That's where he is! In the cemetery!

JOE

I told you. They're burying him! That's what they're doing—they're burying him!

HENDERSON

Will you listen to that bugle? I'm almost ashamed to be
here.
(Shouts off toward the side)
Starkey! Hey, Starkey!
(Starkey rushes out onstage while the bugle is still
playing, rolling a square green bin before him that
rides on wheels. On the side of the bin are lettered
the words: "WEAPONS DIVISION." Starkey's manner
is brisk and enthusiastic as he begins performing
the prescribed functions about which the Major
boasted to the two Sportsmen earlier. He is smoking one of his slim cigars, and he wears his whistle
around his neck)
Whose idea is *that*, for Christ sake! Taps!

(Starkey comes to a stop, removes his hat, and
stands in respectful silence until the bugler fin-
ishes)

STARKEY

That was for Sinclair. They're burying him now.
(Stares with surprise at the men resting on the
ground)
What are you people doing?

(The men are embarrassed)

BAILEY

(Finally)
Pushups.

73

STARKEY

(Dryly)
You'll strain yourself.
(To Henderson)
And what are you doing in that uniform?

HENDERSON

I've been trying to find Sinclair. I'm a little confused about a few things.

STARKEY

You're supposed to be dressed for calisthenics. There's nothing confusing. Sinclair is dead and buried now, and we just go ahead without him.

HENDERSON

But where is he really?

STARKEY

Are you serious?

HENDERSON

I'd like to know.

STARKEY

There is no Sinclair.

HENDERSON

Then how can he be dead and buried?

STARKEY

There never was a Sinclair. He isn't real. I'm not real. I'm not really a captain. I'm pretending, and I'm sure that all of you—

74

(To the audience)

—and all of you out there, have seen me act many, many times before in many different roles. As you know, I've been doing very, very well lately. I've had much bigger parts than this one, and I've also made lots more money than I'm getting here. But I do like to try new things, and I do like to keep in touch with the legitimate American theater. And that's why I consented to act the part of a captain for a while.

(To the men)

Do you understand?

(Bailey and Fisher applaud deadpan. Starkey, missing their sarcasm, is pleased)

BAILEY

That's the hardest part you ever played.

STARKEY

A captain?

BAILEY

No. An actor.

(The men guffaw)

HENDERSON

Starkey—

STARKEY

Captain Starkey.

HENDERSON

About Sinclair.

STARKEY

There *was* no Sinclair. He never lived. He didn't die.

HENDERSON

Then who did we just bury?

STARKEY

Sinclair. But he wasn't real. It didn't happen.

HENDERSON

Why did we bury him?

STARKEY

Because he was killed.

HENDERSON

Where is the boy who was playing the soldier who was killed by accident just now—

STARKEY

Not by accident. There are no accidents.

HENDERSON

By accident. He was killed in my plane when one of his own bombs exploded, wasn't he? That's an accident. He used to be an actor about my own age. He was here a little while ago. He isn't here now.

STARKEY

He isn't supposed to be here. We don't need him any more. That's why we killed him.

HENDERSON

I'm going to look for him.

STARKEY

No, you're not!

HENDERSON

I am.

STARKEY

Not now, you aren't. I need you here to help me distribute this new equipment. You stand right there with the idiots. I'm in charge now. And I'm tired of arguing with you over every little thing that has to be done.

HENDERSON

Then can I go?

STARKEY

Then you can go get into a clean uniform for the trip to Minnesota.

HENDERSON

Minnesota?

STARKEY

Yes, Minnesota. That's your next target, men.

BAILEY

What's in Minnesota?

STARKEY

(Rumpling Bailey's hair)
Your next target. Any questions?

FISHER

Sir? Is this mission to Minnesota going to be dangerous?

STARKEY

Not for those who survive, as I once heard the Major say.
Any other questions?

HENDERSON

Where's Sinclair?

STARKEY

I've already answered that one. And now, everybody up
and on your toes! Hear ye, hear ye! It's time for the
wonderful new equipment that will put you all in just the
right frame of mind for the big mission to Minnesota.

BAILEY

What new equipment?

STARKEY

You'll all love every piece of it.

JOE

Girls?

STARKEY

Oh, shut up, Joe, you old degenerate. This is serious.
    (Opens the bin)
Gather close and listen carefully. Henderson, you'll come
first . . . because *you're* a *sergeant*. Now, men, war isn't
just bullets and bombs. Oh, no. There's such a thing as
the battle for men's minds and souls, including yours, and
we've got in here the equipment that is going to win it.
There's no doubt about that. Are you ready, Henderson—
my protégé, friend, colleague, and good soldier? One . . .
two . . . three!

(Starkey reaches inside the bin and pulls out, holds up, and then flips to Henderson a miniature baseball bat. Henderson is puzzled)

HENDERSON

It's a little baseball bat.

STARKEY

(Grinning)
That's right.

(Henderson flings the bat away furiously)

HENDERSON

We've got a real baseball bat!

(He starts away)

STARKEY

Then how about this?

(With sly amusement, as though relishing what he knows is to come, Starkey pulls out a basketball and lobs it to Henderson. Henderson catches the ball and looks at it with surprise)

HENDERSON

A basketball!

(Starkey nods. Angrily, Henderson flips the ball away. One of the Idiots jumps forward and catches it. He gazes at the ball in dumb puzzlement for a few seconds and then flips it to a second Idiot; and suddenly about four of the men are playing with the basketball intently)

79

STARKEY
Here, Henderson! How's this?

(Starkey pulls out another basketball and lobs it to Henderson, who, with slightly hypnotic bewilderment, catches it)

HENDERSON
It's another basketball!

STARKEY
A replacement. The Major wants us to have lots of replacement parts. Come on, Henderson, play. Play.
(Henderson shakes his head determinedly and flings the ball away. Fisher lunges for it. He tries to dribble around Bailey, then passes off instead to Joe, who dribbles toward the rear a few steps and passes back to Fisher. As Henderson stares and Starkey grins, an orgy of ball playing develops that grows in noise and accelerates in action, with the five Idiots playing most vigorously of all. Starkey next takes out a football and fades back a few steps to pass)
Yo! Come on, Henderson, catch! Play, Henderson, play. Join the team.

(Henderson continues shaking his head. The men let out exclamations of delight when they see the football)

BAILEY
Hey, a football! A football!

(Starkey throws the football toward Henderson. Bailey darts out and makes a nice catch. Proud of himself, Bailey tosses the ball to Henderson and starts running, calling loudly to Henderson for a pass. Henderson hesitates over the ball a moment and then, almost in spite of himself, throws a pass to Bailey, who catches it and flips an underhand pass back to him. And now everyone but Starkey is participating in this play frenzy. Starkey beams with satisfaction and urges them on with loud shouts of encouragement and shrill blasts from his whistle. He watches with pleasure for a few more seconds and then dips happily into the bin again and emerges with both arms filled with children's colored building blocks)

STARKEY

Building blocks!
(Almost maniacally, Starkey showers the building blocks out over the stage. While a few of the men scurry for them, Starkey dips into the bin again and emerges with clusters of baby rattles)
Rattles!
(He showers the baby rattles onto the stage and reaches into the bin again)
Plastic harmonicas!
(Henderson has stopped playing and watches with a look of angry horror. Starkey emerges from the bin again with his hands full)
Pacifiers!

(Starkey flings up the baby pacifiers too. The men, all but Henderson, are all over the stage now playing with the blocks and rattles and pacifiers and plastic harmonicas. Henderson calls out to Starkey in astonishment)

HENDERSON

Starkey! *Starkey!* What the hell are you doing? We're not babies! We're not kids. We're grown-up men!

STARKEY

Are you? Henderson, are you a man? That's good then, because I've got just the game for you grown-up *men*. On your feet, everybody. Everybody up. Form a circle.

(As the men comply, Starkey reaches into the bin and lifts out a toy that is called "Time Bomb." It is black and round and has a stemlike device for winding. Starkey turns the winder rapidly, then tosses the bomb to one of the men)

Okay, pass it around! Fast. Keep it moving!

(Uncertainly, the man with the bomb tosses it to someone else, and the men begin passing it from one to the other)

JOE

What is it? Captain, what is it?

STARKEY

It's a toy. It's called "Time Bomb." It's a game, just like musical chairs. Keep it moving—fast, faster! Whoever's got it when the bell rings, loses.

(The men fall readily into the spirit of the game once they understand, and they toss the bomb back and forth like a hot potato. After a few seconds, a bell inside the bomb goes off loudly. The man holding the bomb grins sheepishly; the others taunt him good-naturedly)

JOE

Hey, this is pretty good. Let's play some more.

STARKEY

I'm glad you like it. Because I've got another one for you. Put that one down.

(Starkey takes out a second one, winds it, and tosses it out to start the game again. The men play with freer enjoyment and zeal, tossing the bomb from one to the other with shouts and laughter. In a little while, the bell goes off. But this time, as soon as the bell rings, Starkey speaks sharply to the man holding the bomb)

Throw it! Quick! Get rid of it! Throw it away! *Throw it!*

(The man freezes with terror for an instant, then finally reacts. He turns, pulls his arm back, and hurls the bomb far away into the wings. Immediately, there is a tremendous explosion from where the bomb has vanished. Fire flashes and smoke billows out onto the stage; and the men, all but Starkey, hit the floor, a few as though for safety, the rest as though staggered by the concussion. For a few seconds, they are utterly without motion, all but Starkey, who, wearing a smile, drifts back toward the toy bin. Bailey and Henderson spring up in rage)

BAILEY

Hey, what the hell's the idea?

HENDERSON

Starkey—you son of a bitch! You want to kill us? What—

STARKEY

Hold it! The Major wants me to give you one more.
Everybody up. Up.
> (Starkey takes another bomb from the bin and
> begins to wind it. The men rise slowly and draw
> away from him in a wider circle than before)

One more time. Okay? Everybody ready and willing?
Good. Keep it moving, boys. Remember—keep it moving.

> (Starkey tosses the bomb out, and the game begins
> again. This time, though, the men are rigid with
> fear and fling the bomb away as quickly as they
> can. An air of panic grows steadily)

FISHER

Captain Starkey, sir. Please—

> (The bomb is tossed to Fisher and he has to break
> off to catch it and throw it to somebody else)

JOE

Sir? Sir? Which one is this? Is it the toy or is it the
bomb?

STARKEY

> (Laughing)

Boys, that's where the real fun comes in. *I don't know!*
> (The men go almost wild with fear now as they
> pass the bomb around from one to the other rapidly.
> Finally the bell sounds. The man holding the bomb
> lets out a wailing gasp. In vivid terror, he tosses the
> bomb to Henderson. Startled, Henderson utters a
> loud cry and throws the bomb to Starkey. Starkey
> catches it and is thunderstruck to find himself
> holding it. He seems paralyzed. After an instant
> more of shocked bewilderment, he rushes toward

the front of the stage, and, letting out a terrified scream, draws his arm back to hurl the ringing time bomb out into the audience.

Suddenly, in mid-motion, Starkey stops, chuckles pleasantly, and relaxes entirely. Holding the bomb up harmlessly, Starkey continues moving toward the front of the stage with a comfortable, reassuring smile and addresses the audience, obviously enjoying the role he is playing now)

It's okay, folks. This is not a real bomb, and nobody here is going to get hurt. Not yet. We're not really going to blow you up. So we can all relax because it's only a toy, isn't it?

(Grinning and chuckling in the friendliest fashion, he stands there a moment. Then, with a brief scream, he pulls back suddenly in a gesture of mock horror and tosses the bomb off the stage onto the floor in front of the first row of spectators. He laughs again at this new prank and turns back to speak to the men on stage)

Okay, men. You can take a break now. Ten minutes.

(To the audience)

You, too.

(Approaches Henderson and speaks to him tauntingly)

And, Henderson—try to be on time once, will you? We'll need you very quickly for that mission to Minnesota.

(Starkey signals, and the curtain begins to close)

Oh, and all of you—get that junk out of here.

(Starkey takes his portfolio and his newspaper from inside the bin and walks away with a carefree wave to the audience. The men stare after him a moment and then sink down to begin picking up the toys and balls as the curtain closes quickly)

ACT

Two

○ ○ ○ ○ ○ ○ ○

T HE CURTAIN opens on a silent and empty
stage. The balls and toys have been removed.

After a precisely measured pause of ten seconds, a low rumble is heard backstage; then a
black bowling ball (or a bowling ball exactly the
same color as the toy time bombs used in the preceding act) rolls out from one side of the stage
at normal bowling speed. It rolls clear across the
stage and goes out of sight into the wings on the
other side. After another second or two, there is
heard from offstage that unmistakable sound of
pins being struck in a bowling alley.

The echo dies away. There is absolute silence
for about another five seconds. Then the black
bowling ball appears again, rolling back across
stage from the other direction, this time at a
slightly slower speed. The ball rolls out of sight,
and the noise it is making dies after another second or two.

There is another pause of almost ten seconds.
Then the bowling ball is rolled out again.

At just about the same time, Fisher and Fisher's Kid Brother walk out onstage from the direction toward which the bowling ball is rolling. Fisher is dressed in his combat uniform. Fisher's Kid Brother wears civilian clothes appropriate to his age and the current local fashion. He is very young, perhaps no more than twelve or thirteen.

The bowling ball rolls by them and disappears offstage. After another few seconds, there is heard again the hollow, echoing noise of bowling pins being knocked down.

YOUNG FISHER
(Reacting to the noise)
What was that?

FISHER
(Looks offstage)
A spare.

(They advance to center stage, Young Fisher staring all about with a look of wide-eyed amazement)

YOUNG FISHER
Is this where it all happens?
(Fisher nods)
Where are the planes and the bombs and the targets?

FISHER
Oh, that's all out there someplace. All the fighting takes place far away.

YOUNG FISHER
(Referring to the audience)
They don't see it?

FISHER

No, they wouldn't like that. There's no violence out here, and no blood. Nobody gets killed here, so you don't have to worry. There's no violence in public.

YOUNG FISHER

There's lots of violence in Shakespeare.

FISHER

Shakespeare had a low audience. We've got a high audience. We're all here for a good time. That's why we've got all those guns and toys.

YOUNG FISHER

Can I play with the bowling ball?

FISHER

That's just for officers.

YOUNG FISHER

Can I make a speech? To them?

FISHER

Sure. If you do it before anyone comes. Go ahead.

(Young Fisher steps forward hesitantly toward the audience)

YOUNG FISHER

(To Fisher)
What should I say? –

FISHER

Say thanks.

YOUNG FISHER

For what?

FISHER

For letting you come here. You can thank them all for letting you come here and be a soldier.

YOUNG FISHER

(Stricken with shyness)

No.

FISHER

Say hello. Go ahead. It's just like talking into a telephone.
    (Young Fisher shakes his head bashfully and starts
    to drift back)
I'll show you.
    (Steps forward to address the audience)
Hello?
    (Listens a moment and turns back to his brother)
See? It's just like talking into a telephone.

YOUNG FISHER

Maybe later. Where's everyone else?

FISHER

They'll be here soon. Wait till you see the way we all get going. It's a riot. Look . . . look!
    (Two men burst suddenly onstage, struggling
    earnestly and violently for possession of a basket-
    ball)
That's an idiot!

YOUNG FISHER

Which one?

FISHER

I can't tell.

(The two men pull apart angrily. One of them, an Idiot, has the ball and guards it defiantly. The other man is Joe. Joe snarls at the Idiot)

JOE

Aah, to hell with you.
(To Fisher)
Where's Bailey? Where's Henderson?
(Calling across stage into the wings)
Hey, Bailey! Hey, Henderson! Who's got a goddam ball?

(Another Idiot comes on with a basketball. Joe grabs it away from him triumphantly, and Fisher and Fisher's Kid Brother laugh with amusement and applaud)

JOE

Hey, who's this?

FISHER

My kid brother.

JOE

Welcome aboard, kid. Catch.

(Joe bounces the ball to Young Fisher, who handles it uncertainly for a few seconds and then passes or kicks the ball to the motioning Idiot. Other members of the cast begin streaming in from different directions, all back in their combat outfits and each busy with a ball or a toy from the preceding scene.
One or two of the Idiots enter, shaking baby rat-

tles like maracas, and another plays quite well on one of the plastic harmonicas. From the other side, Bailey runs straight out on stage at top speed, turns sharply, and looks back in time to catch a football thrown to him from the wings. Another Idiot enters, balancing a tower of building blocks. A moment later Ruth enters from the other side, balancing a tower of donuts on a wooden stick, and heads across stage. She pauses a moment to regard the activity of the others. She sees that no one is noticing her and steps forward toward the footlights to address the audience. She pauses furtively to look around again and then begins reciting hurriedly, as though knowing she is not going to get very far)

RUTH

(With gestures and magniloquence, brandishing her spire of donuts as though it were a sword)
"Once more unto the breach, dear friends, once more; Or close the wall up with our English dead."

BAILEY

(Truly angry)
Hey, get out of here! That's my speech, you little bitch!
(As Ruth retreats and exits petulantly)
"Once more unto the—"

FISHER

No, it isn't. It's Captain Starkey's.

BAILEY

Well, it isn't hers! "Once more—"

YOUNG FISHER

I could do *that* one. "Once more unto the—"

BAILEY

You better not try!
    (While they argue, the bowling ball comes rolling back suddenly across the stage. Just before the ball disappears on the other side, Henderson steps out onstage near its path and turns to watch it roll by. Henderson has a baby pacifier in his mouth and munches on it for effect as he waits to be noticed. His expression is ironic and resentful. Under his arm, he conceals and grips something the same way he might hold a football. Bailey steps forward toward the footlights to begin reciting heroically again)
"Once more unto the breach, dear friends—"
    (Spies Henderson)
Hey! Where can *I* get one of those nipples?

HENDERSON

Run, Bailey. Run out for a pass, like the great athlete you think you are.

    (Bailey darts away eagerly)

BAILEY

Throw it! Throw it!

    (Henderson fades back like an experienced ballplayer and cocks his arm to throw; what he is holding is now seen to be some rolled-up garments. Henderson lofts the garments toward Bailey as he would pass a football. They come apart in midair and fall to the floor. Bailey holds them up in surprise, a pair of trousers, a sports shirt, and an old pair of shoes)

BAILEY

What's this?

HENDERSON

(Sardonically)
Don't you recognize him?

BAILEY

Who?

HENDERSON

Sinclair. Don't you remember Sinclair? Our friend? Our contemporary? The one that didn't want to go on the mission to Constantinople. That's all that's left of him. That's all I could find.

JOE

You mean he left with his uniform?

HENDERSON

I mean he left with his boots on, if he left at all.
(Cups his hands around his mouth and calls out into the theater at the top of his voice)
Sinclair!
(He listens a second or two and turns back to the others)
See? No answer.

YOUNG FISHER

Who's Sinclair?

94

FISHER

He's the fellow you're replacing. He was killed on the mission to Constantinople a little while ago.

HENDERSON

And those are his remains. Two rags.

YOUNG FISHER

(Finally finding the courage to address the audience)
"Those are pearls that were his eyes."

HENDERSON

Hey, who the hell are *you*?

(The boy retreats from Henderson in fear. Joe spies something offstage and points with surprise, grinning)

JOE

Look at that! Hey, will you look at that!

BAILEY

Well I'll be damned! Make way for the army.
(Marches comically in place)
Hut . . . hut . . . hut, hut, hut!

(While the others all stare with amusement, the two Sportsmen march happily out onstage, counting exuberant military cadence of their own. They still carry the golf club and the shotgun. From the waist up, they are dressed now in MP uniforms; from the waist down they still wear respectively the golfing and hunting attire in which they were last seen, and the total effect of their marching and

95

costume is to give them an incongruous and totally ridiculous appearance. A few of the men let out taunting shouts and fall in behind them in jeering emulation, making fun)

BOTH SPORTSMEN

Left . . . left . . . left, right, left!

GOLFER

You had a good home when you left!

HUNTER

You're right!

GOLFER

Your mother was sad when you left!

HUNTER

You're right!

GOLFER

Sound off!

HUNTER

One, two!

GOLFER

Hit it again!

HUNTER

Three, four!

GOLFER

Change count!

(Others, all but Henderson, join in)

ALL

One, two, three, four, one two . . . three, four!

(With Bailey taking charge, the men begin trooping around in a carefree parade, singing a marching song into which Bailey has led them. The Sportsmen are beside themselves with joy to find themselves taking part in a parade. The others burlesque them. As they march and sing, Henderson roams the stage morosely, calling out searchingly into the wings and theater from time to time)

HENDERSON

Sinclair! *Sinclair!* Where the hell are you?

(Suddenly, Fisher spies something offstage and yells out a frantic warning)

FISHER

Hey, cheese it fellows. Hold it, hold it!

A few of the men come to attention and wait with eyes askance. From the direction in which they look, the Major walks slowly onstage, carrying a bowling ball in a bowling ball bag and dressed completely in the uniform of a member of a bowling team. When he turns, the insignia and name of a bowling team can be seen on the back of his jacket. Like Henderson, the Major also is munching on a baby pacifier.

At the sight of the Major, the rest of the men grow silent and still, all but the Idiots, who keep on with the singing and marching until it finally dawns on them that the others have stopped, and then their voices trail away.

Munching on his pacifier, the Major moves along the line of men, studying them. He approaches and comes face-to-face finally with Henderson at the other end, and the two men stare at each other in silence a few seconds, pacifier to pacifier)

MAJOR

(Removes his pacifier).
Henderson?

HENDERSON

(Removes his)
Sir?

MAJOR

What's going on here?

(Henderson shrugs uncomfortably)

GOLFER

We're just having a little parade.

BAILEY

While we're getting together.

FISHER

And waiting to begin again.

HUNTER

That's all.

GOLFER

Just a little parade.

· Act TWO ·

(The Major addresses the two Sportsmen affably)

MAJOR

I see. That's all right. Well? Do you like what you're doing here?

SPORTSMEN

And how!

MAJOR

That's good.
(Adjusts the MP band on the arm of one)
Let's see what you've learned so far. You two only—
Attention! Right face! Left face! Present arms! Shoulder arms! Port arms! Ready!
(The Sportsmen respond efficiently to each order. At this last command, issued in a louder voice, each assumes a position appropriate to the implement he is carrying. The Golfer turns to the side and takes the stance of a man about to tee off. The Hunter extends his shotgun in the manner of a skeet-shooter waiting for the target to appear. The Major observes them for a second or two)
Aim!
(At this command, the Golfer swings his club back and up and holds his position. The Hunter aims his shotgun and waits alertly for the Major to issue his next command)
Fire!
(The Golfer swings; and the Hunter, a moment afterward, speaks)

HUNTER

Bang.

99

MAJOR

Very, very good.
    (To the others)
Right?
    (The others nod in perfunctory agreement)
Now . . . double-time . . . march! Hut . . . two . . . three
. . . four . . .
    (The Sportsmen begin trotting offstage. A second
    or so before the Sportsmen disappear, the Major
    begins clapping his hands, applauding their per-
    formance. He signals to the other men, and they
    begin clapping too. After the Sportsmen go, the
    Major turns, still clapping, to include the men in
    his approval also. He stops. The men continue
    clapping their hands for a few more seconds before
    they take notice of the glowering look on the
    Major's face and realize that he wants them to
    stop applauding too)
Very good. All of you. Where's Starkey?

BAILEY

I think he's with his wife now.
    (Points after Ruth)
She just went that way.

MAJOR

Henderson?

HENDERSON

Sir?

MAJOR

You take charge of them till Starkey gets here.

HENDERSON

Yes, sir!

MAJOR

Do you know what to do?

HENDERSON

Oh, yes indeed, sir. I certainly do. I can handle it all. I could do everything the captain does. I could take over for him right now if you wanted me to.

MAJOR

I *don't* want you to. I only want you to keep them going until the captain gets here, and that's all I want you to do. Do you understand?

HENDERSON

(Backing away in humiliation)
Yes, sir.

MAJOR

Carry on, then.

HENDERSON

Yes, sir.

(The Major glares at him a moment longer and begins walking away. Henderson, sulking with disappointment, puts the pacifier back in his mouth. The Major turns slowly back toward him with a look of contempt)

MAJOR

And by the way, Henderson. Take that silly thing out of

your mouth and start acting your age. There's nothing really funny about this, you know.

(Henderson removes the pacifer from his mouth and looks meekly for some place to dispose of it. Finally, he shoves it into his pocket)

HENDERSON

(Sheepishly)
Yes, sir.
(The Major glares at him a moment longer with blunt satisfaction. Then, almost without realizing what he is doing, he puts his own pacifier back in his mouth, turns, and continues offstage.
    The men are motionless until the Major has gone. Then, all at once, they launch themselves into snarling and obscene gestures of anger and resentment. Then they separate and sprawl out on the ground. A few light cigarettes. Henderson is angriest of all)
God, I hate that bastard! I really do. When I stop to think about him, I hate him!

YOUNG FISHER

What's wrong with him?

(Young Fisher has seated himself on a basketball. Henderson whirls furiously and kicks the ball out from under him)

HENDERSON

(Harshly)
Say, who the hell *are* you anyway?
(Relenting immediately, he helps the frightened

boy to his feet and tries apologetically to calm him)
I'm sorry. Forgive me—I'm sorry. Who the hell are ya,
kid? Really? What are you doing here?

FISHER

He's my baby brother. He's part of our company now.

HENDERSON

Him? He's so young.
    (Touches the back of his fingers to the boy's face,
      as though feeling for some sign of a beard)
You're just a little kid, aren't you?

YOUNG FISHER

    (Seriously)
They said that the younger they took me into the service,
the better it would be for me. They said it would disrupt
my life less if I got killed sooner.

HENDERSON

Well, I'll be damned. They want a kid, so they get a kid.
They want some idiots, so they get some real ones.
    (Scanning the Idiots)
That's something I'm still not sure of. Are you idiots
really idiots, or aren't you?
    (The Idiots regard him in expressionless silence,
      giving no clue at all)
No help.
    (To the audience)
They're pretty good, aren't they—for a bunch of idiots!
    (Speaking to the Idiots)
You know, I'm starting to figure something out. You five
idiots are either very smart or very dumb. If you're very
smart, you wouldn't be here with us. But you are here with

us, so that means you're very dumb. But we're not very dumb, are we, and we're here with you. We're pretty bright, in fact. We're much smarter than you, but here we are *with* you. So that means we may be much dumber than you after all, doesn't it? Doesn't it?

(One of the Idiots giggles)

Hey, listen to *him*! Next thing you know they'll all begin talking. *Then* what a time we'll have trying to figure out who's in charge. Everybody's got big ambitions around here. Especially Rudolph, who wants to be a sergeant and take my place. Right, Bailey, boy?

BAILEY

Yeah, what about you just now when you thought you had a chance to be captain?

(Jumps up and does a derisive imitation of Henderson earlier)

Oh, yes, sir, Major, sir. I can handle it all, sir. I can do everything the captain does if you wanted me to, sir. Yes, sir, no, sir, no, sir, yes, sir.

(Henderson advances upon him in anger and embarrassment)

HENDERSON

How would you like a punch in the face?

(Bailey is not intimidated and faces him aggressively)

BAILEY

You just try it, buddy. You just try it and I'll throw you the hell out into the eighth row center.

(Henderson is startled by Bailey's response and already sorry for his own truculence)

HENDERSON

Okay. Okay.

BAILEY

Don't get carried away by those sergeant's stripes. They're only decorations.

HENDERSON

Okay, I said. I said okay, didn't I? Everybody's turning very mean around here suddenly, aren't we?

JOE

It's a war, kid. I told you that.

FISHER

Why don't you two guys shake hands and be friends? Haven't we got enough fighting to do?

BAILEY

Okay. You want to?

(Henderson grins, and he and Bailey shake hands, a bit self-consciously, and jostle each other lightly in some awkward horseplay)

JOE

Hey, Henderson. You're supposed to get busy now. The Major said you should keep things going until Captain Starkey gets here.

HENDERSON

Let Starkey do his own work. He's getting all the credit.

(Henderson and the others settle down comfortably on the floor)

YOUNG FISHER

Is this all we do?

FISHER

Just for a little while. Then we've got some real good
things coming up.

HENDERSON

(Sarcastically)

Sure, some wonderful things. War can be a pretty beautiful experience . . . if you're on the winning side and you
don't get hurt. I was killed once, a long time ago, in a play
called *Journey's End*.

BAILEY

Hey, I saw you in that.

HENDERSON

Yeah, I know—I stank.

BAILEY

No—you had some good moments.

HENDERSON

(Smiles, acknowledging the joke)

But I didn't mind getting killed then, because it was all in
fun. That whole war was all in fun, if I remember cor-
rectly, but I forget which war it was.

JOE

(To Young Fisher)

Aah, don't mind him. Look, kid, you joined up with us at
a very good time.

FISHER

We go on leave soon.

HENDERSON

(Caustically)
And get more medals and more money.

BAILEY

And I get promoted.

JOE

We have lots of dames and lots of booze.

FISHER

We visit the best cities in the world.

HENDERSON

Before we destroy them.

BAILEY

And I get promoted.

FISHER

In Rome, we see the Colosseum.

BAILEY

Just once.

JOE

And then we go dancing and loving with those beautiful
Italian girls.

FISHER

We visit St. Peter's.

BAILEY

Just once.

JOE

And then it's back to those beautiful girls. Hey, Henderson,
remember the fun we used to have—you, me, and those
beautiful girls?
　　(Joe laughs, draws a deep breath, and begins sing-
　　ing softly)
"Roll me over,
In the clover,
Roll me over, lay me down, and do it again."

HENDERSON

　　(Remembering with enthusiasm)
Yeah, yeah, yeah—I've got to admit that. Kid, they've got
these big things built in Naples that will knock your eyes
out. They're called . . . *hookers*.

BAILEY

In Paris—

FISHER

We visit the Louvre.

BAILEY

Just once! And then I flop into bed with one of those
beautiful French cuties and really make love—

HENDERSON

Just once!

　　(Bailey and the others laugh)

BAILEY

Hey, I make the jokes here. You make the speeches.

HENDERSON

Yeah. And you get promoted.

JOE

(Enumerating on his fingers)
We have sex orgies in New York, New Haven, Los Angeles—

BAILEY

No—we bombed in New Haven three weeks ago.

HENDERSON

(Sarcastically clapping his hands)
Good for *us*. We bombed in New Haven.

FISHER

Three weeks ago, it was Philadelphia.

BAILEY

Boston.

JOE

Amsterdam. And Stockholm, Sweden.

FISHER

Denver, Colorado.

HENDERSON

And next, it's Minnesota. *That's* our business now. You want to know who I really am? You want to know what I really do?

(Young Fisher nods enthusiastically, and Henderson begins singing. The others join in, and they romp boisterously through a song for Young Fisher's amusement)

109

SONG

"With my feet on the glass,
And my head up my ass,
I just go bomb, bomb, bombing along.

It's easy to rate,
When you're dropping 'em straight,
And just keep bomb, bomb bombing along.

With plenty of hits,
And a low C.E.
Oh, what Saint Peter
Will do to me!

We've got our feet on the glass,
And our head up our ass,
As we go bomb, bomb, bombing along."

BAILEY

"Let's drop a spitball."

ALL

"As we go bomb, bomb, bombing along."

(The song ends with laughter and with exaggerated bows and other gestures of self-congratulation. Henderson rumples Young Fisher's hair and speaks with a big grin)

HENDERSON

Oh, yes. I've got to admit that. We are going to have a hell of a good time.

BAILEY

But first we've got to fly that mission to Minnesota.

JOE

(To Henderson)
And you get killed.

(The grin on Henderson's face freezes, then turns
slowly into a frown)

HENDERSON

I do?

JOE

Sure.

BAILEY

That's why *I* get promoted.

HENDERSON

That's right, I do. Son of a bitch! I really gotta die? Now?

BAILEY

Sure. You and you—Fisher—and one of the idiots, that big
one with the blond hair. Right?

(At this, Fisher looks confused. Joe begins moving
stealthily away to the side)

HENDERSON

I'm gonna be dead—so soon? Finished? Out of it all? Just
like that?

FISHER

(Rousing himself)
Hey, wait a minute! Wait a minute! I'm not the one who
gets killed now!

I I I

(To Joe)
You're the one who gets killed now. Aren't you?

JOE

(Somberly)
Yeah. I was kind of hoping you wouldn't notice the difference. I'd like to be around a little longer too, even though I'm getting old.

HENDERSON

I'm not gonna go.

BAILEY

You've gotta go. How else can I get promoted?

HENDERSON

You mean I'm really supposed to go out now and get killed? Just like Sinclair?

BAILEY

Oh, no. He got wounded and bled to death. You blow up ... in a big explosion ... right over the field, where *everybody* can hear you.

HENDERSON

And then you're all gonna go out and have a good time? After I'm dead?

BAILEY

What do you want? You're not the only person who ever got killed in a war.

HENDERSON

Well, Jesus Christ. I'd like to have something happen after

I'm gone—something to show that I'd been here once. I'd like to be remembered. Really, I would.

BAILEY

You'll be remembered. We'll even talk about you once in a while. Just like we talk about Sinclair.

JOE

Will you talk about me, too?

BAILEY

Sure, Joe. Why not?

HENDERSON

(Bitterly)

Yeah. I know how we miss Sinclair. I'm the only one that even looks for him. Aren't you even gonna be sad?

FISHER

I'll be sad.

BAILEY

Just once.

HENDERSON

And then?

BAILEY

We have fun.

HENDERSON

Oh, great. While I'm lying out there dead.

BAILEY

What do you want us to do? Hold services forever?

HENDERSON

(Indicates audience)
What about them? Are they gonna care if I get killed?

BAILEY

Why should they? That's what they came to see.

HENDERSON

Did they? Well, it's too bad about them. Look what happened to Sinclair.

BAILEY

What happened to Sinclair?

HENDERSON

I don't know what happened to Sinclair!
(Fumbles through Sinclair's shirt and trousers and shoes as though searching for him there and then calls out again)
Sinclair!
(Listens a moment, hears no response, and then tosses the clothes away)
I'm not gonna do it!

BAILEY

Goddammit—I want my promotion! You've got to fly to Minnesota, and you've got to be killed.

HENDERSON

Who says so?

BAILEY

I say so. And the Major says so.

114

HENDERSON

Well, I'll tell you something.
(To the audience)
I'll tell you all something.
(To audience and the men on stage)
I'm not going to go out now and get killed just because you
all expect me to. I don't like the Major. And I suddenly
don't like any part of this, either. Because after I get killed,
you get killed, and after you get killed, you get killed, and
after—

YOUNG FISHER

Me? I just got here.

HENDERSON

So what? Why the hell do you think they got you here?
And after you get killed—

BAILEY

I get promoted.

HENDERSON

You get promoted! Big deal! You get promoted! And after
you get promoted, then what do you get?

BAILEY

(Puzzled)
Killed?

HENDERSON

How should I know? By that time I'm already dead and
gone . . . and forgotten, too!

BAILEY

I don't care! I want my promotion, anyway. I don't know what I want! But I know I want my promotion!

HENDERSON

You want your promotion! Well, that's just too bad. This is a stupid part in a stupid show, and I'm not going ahead with it!

> (Bailey stares at Henderson in astonishment. After a second, Joe and one of the Idiots begin applauding)

BAILEY

What are you applauding for?

JOE

> (Glumly)

If he don't go, I can't go. I don't want to die yet, either.

BAILEY

> (To Idiot)

What are *you* applauding for?

> (The Idiot doesn't answer)

HENDERSON

Leave him alone. He's learning, that's why! He's not such an idiot after all!

BAILEY

Okay, I don't care. It's not my worry. Let everything stop. Just sit here and do nothing and see what happens when Starkey comes.

HENDERSON

What happens when Starkey comes?

BAILEY

I straighten up and holler—

(Fisher jumps to his feet)

FISHER

Attention!

BAILEY

(Pushes Fisher roughly and angrily)
Hey, I'm supposed to say that! What the hell are you stealing my line for? Attention!

(Bailey and a few of the others stand up at attention. Henderson does not. Starkey strolls in, smiling pleasantly, chewing on a piece from a donut he holds in one hand. In his other hand, he carries his portfolio and his newspaper)

STARKEY

Hey, up, up. You're all supposed to be at attention when I walk in.
(Senses something amiss)
What's wrong?

BAILEY

There's a slight rebellion in progress. A kind of insurrection.

STARKEY

What kind of rebellion?

BAILEY

Ask him.

STARKEY

(To Henderson)
What kind of rebellion?

HENDERSON

Ask him.

STARKEY

Come on, fellas, we've got work to do. There's no more
time for games.

BAILEY

It's him. He doesn't want to go to Minnesota and get killed.

STARKEY

Why not?

HENDERSON

Why not?

STARKEY

Yeah, why not? Why don't you want to get killed?

HENDERSON

What are you eating?

STARKEY

A donut.

HENDERSON

That's why not. How come you have a donut now and I
don't?

STARKEY

Oh, Jesus, is that all? If I give you the donut, will you go get killed?

HENDERSON

You've *got* the donut. So *you* get killed.

STARKEY

It isn't even a good donut. Listen, Henderson—I'm sorry if I've been picking on you and criticizing you, and I'm sorry if the two of us don't like each other and don't get along. But you haven't exactly been making things easy for me, either, you know. Let's try to keep personal feelings out of this. We've both got a job to do. You've got yours, and I've got mine.

HENDERSON

Your job is better than mine.

FISHER

You get the donut.

JOE

You get the girl.

HENDERSON

You probably even get good coffee.

STARKEY

Well, we all can't have everything.

HENDERSON

Say, that's a swell line. We oughta bomb that line instead of Minnesota.

STARKEY

Now you're getting rotten again.

HENDERSON

Let's change jobs now, you and me.

STARKEY

Oh, no. Not a chance. I like my job. I kind of like my job here an awful lot, Henderson. And that's why I'm just not going to let you jeopardize it. I'm going to keep giving you orders. And you're going to keep right on obeying them. Because I kind of like things here just the way they are.

HENDERSON

Is that right? Why should I have to go out and die now while you and the Major live? Is that fair?

STARKEY

Who cares whether it's "fair" or not? You've got to go out now and destroy Minnesota before it's too late.

HENDERSON

Too late for what?

STARKEY

Well . . . too late to destroy it, I guess. Henderson, my friend—
     (Slips an arm around Henderson's shoulders)
—let me advise you, once more just—
     (Almost without realizing it, Starkey begins to re-
     cite, turning into an actor consciously playing a
     cherished role)
"Once more unto the breach, dear friend, once more;"

120

HENDERSON

Are you queer?

STARKEY

(Surprised)
No, of course not.
    (Reciting)
"Or close the wall up with our English dead."
    (Speaking normally)
Why do you ask?

HENDERSON

Why do you have your arm around me?

STARKEY

Huh? Just to be kind of friendly to you . . . you know,
fatherly . . . to speak to you like a father to a son.

HENDERSON

(Coldly)
I don't want you to.

    (Starkey removes his arm and shrugs)

STARKEY

Okay. Why not?

HENDERSON

I've already had a father. I don't trust *you*, either.

STARKEY

You *can* trust me. I'm not a liar. And I'm not a phony or a
hypocrite. Henderson, let me tell you something as an
older and wiser man, something sincere that comes right
from the heart.

(Carried away again by the opportunity to perform, Starkey begins reciting)
"In peace there's nothing so becomes a man
As modest stillness and humility;
But when the blast of war blows in our ears,
Then imitate the action of the tiger!"
(Starkey breaks off abruptly when he notices that the men are listening with expressions that are impassive and scornful)
What's the matter? Don't you like what I'm saying?

HENDERSON

I do it better.

BAILEY

Even your wife does it better.

STARKEY

I'm not doing this for effect, you know.
(There is a shade too much of the histrionic in Starkey's denial; and the men react with catcalls and jeers. Starkey continues heatedly, but soon reverts to his manner of pompous and pedantic recitation)
Do you know what the Roman emperor Augustus Caesar said just before he died? He called it The Comedy of Life. "Remember," said the Emperor Augustus, as he lay on his deathbed, "that you are an actor in a play, the character of which is determined by the Playwright."

BAILEY

That great playwright in the sky.

(Starkey frowns, but goes on)

STARKEY

"If he wishes the play to be short, it is short; if long, it is long; if He wishes you to play the part of a beggar, remember to act even this role adroitly; and so if your role be that of a cripple, an official, or a layman. For this is your business, to play admirably the role assigned you—"

HENDERSON

Especially if it's the role of an emperor.

JOE

Or a Major.

HENDERSON

Or even a captain.

STARKEY

"—but the selection of that role is another's." And then Augustus asked those around him if he had played well the comedy of life. And when they nodded—

HENDERSON

Of course they nodded. He was the emperor.

STARKEY

—and when they nodded, Augustus added: "Since well I've played my part, all clap your hands. And from the stage dismiss me with applause."

(The Idiots applaud, and Starkey starts to bow. Henderson's sharp question stops him)

HENDERSON

How old was the Emperor Augustus when he died?

STARKEY

Seventy-seven.

HENDERSON

Let *me* live till seventy-seven, and *I'll* play well the comedy of life.

(Starkey is stopped a moment by the request. He answers earnestly)

STARKEY

I can't . . . do that.

HENDERSON

Let me live ten more years. Can you promise me that?

STARKEY

I can't promise.

HENDERSON

One more year.

STARKEY

It can't be done.

HENDERSON

One more hour?

STARKEY

It's too late.

HENDERSON

Will you let me live until ———?

(He names the exact time at which the play might
   be expected to end)
Until the curtain finally comes down?

STARKEY

It's too late.

HENDERSON

And you're advising me to go?

STARKEY

You have to go.

HENDERSON

Are you telling me that now as a father? Or as a captain?
Or as an actor? Or as a friend?

STARKEY

I'm telling it to you as a man.

HENDERSON

That's a crooked answer.

STARKEY

I have no other.

HENDERSON

Then I'll quit.

STARKEY

You can't quit. It's against the rules.

HENDERSON

Change the rules.

125

STARKEY

It's too late for that, too. You're in too deep. We've all gone too far. It's too late for any more of this argument, too. Come on, before the Major gets here.

(Claps his hands to rouse the men)

Let's go, all of you! We've got work to do. We've got one more city to bomb and a million more men to kill.

(To Henderson)

You, too. When you've been in this business as long as I have, you'll learn that the moving finger writes, and having writ—

HENDERSON

Pokes you in the eye.

STARKEY

—moves on! On! On your toes, men! On your feet! On with the scenery. Let's get cracking! Where's that wall? Where's that door? Where's the Major's office? Bring them all on! On with the show! There's the rub, my lad. The play's the thing, and the play must go on. So pitch in now with the others—get going!—and give us our bombs and our benches and our maps and our briefing room.

(Slowly at first, but with increasing zeal, the men rise and get busy bringing out the props and scenery that create the briefing room of Act One. Starkey observes with pleasure as they respond. He begins to hum. They are engaged in doing exactly what they were doing when the curtain rose prematurely to begin the play. Even Henderson gets busy. Young Fisher stands around awkwardly a moment and then approaches Starkey)

126

YOUNG FISHER

Sir? Sir, I don't know what to do.

STARKEY

Who are you?

FISHER

(Calling out)
He's my baby brother.

STARKEY

Just pitch in anywhere and help out. Over there.

YOUNG FISHER

Yes, sir. Sir?

STARKEY

What is it?

YOUNG FISHER

Are you going to kill me, too?

STARKEY

(Arrested by the question)
What?

YOUNG FISHER

Are you going to kill me, too?

STARKEY

Who?

YOUNG FISHER

You, sir.

127

STARKEY

When?

YOUNG FISHER

Now.

STARKEY

Me? No, of course not. I don't kill anybody. We won't kill you until we have to. Go help the others.

YOUNG FISHER

Thank you, sir.

(Young Fisher runs eagerly back to help the men setting up the back wall. Starkey turns from him with relief, only to have his attention beckoned by Ruth, who steps out on stage timidly. Starkey reacts to her with frantic alarm)

RUTH

Starkey! Hey, Starkey!

STARKEY

Ruthie, honey! What the hell are *you* doing out here?

RUTH

Can I come out again and say something?

STARKEY

No, darling, you can't! You're all finished now.

RUTH

Can't I even bring a cup of coffee to the Major?

STARKEY

You did that once!

RUTH

I thought of something new.

STARKEY

There isn't time. Go away now.

RUTH

(Looking around)
What's going on?

STARKEY

We're getting ready to bomb Minnesota.

RUTH

This is more important. Listen—
　　(She dodges past Starkey as he tries to restrain
　　her)
Let me try it out!
　　(She straightens regally, as though preparing to
　　deliver a line of immense dramatic import. Finally,
　　she does speak)
I've got a pie in the oven.

　　(Starkey is incredulous. He smiles with astonish-
　　ment in spite of himself)

STARKEY

A pie in the oven? *A pie in the oven?* Oh, Ruthie, Ruthie.
Get out of here, please! And let me do my work. I've got a
nice job here and I'd like to keep it.

(Ruth gives up. She comes into his arms and they
kiss quickly)

RUTH

When'll I see you?

STARKEY

I'll see you home. Or back in your room, if you want to
wait. But get out of here now—before the Major comes.

(Ruth frowns as Starkey begins leading her offstage. In haste, she pulls away from Starkey to
make a final address to the audience)

RUTH

Thank you. Thank you all for everything. And good-bye.
You've been a wonderful audience. And this has been a
wonderful occasion for me. I want to thank every one of
you for making it possible for me to be here to receive
this wonderful honor, and I want to give credit to everyone connected with this for—I could not have done it
without them!

(Ruth's last words rise to a scream, for Starkey
manages to seize her while she curtsies, and he
pulls her out of sight with him into the wings as
she is speaking.

Starkey returns a few seconds later, shaking his
head indulgently. He starts back toward the center
to continue supervising the setting of the scene.
The last elements of the set are being pushed into
place.

The Major, back in his military uniform, strides
out from the other side, carrying his script again.
He seems in a great hurry.

In other parts of the stage, the other men are rushing about putting the final touches on the set they have assembled, working in a way that becomes almost an exact repetition of the opening moments of the first scene)

MAJOR

Starkey?

STARKEY

Yes, sir.

MAJOR

Have them stay right here when they're finished. I don't want to lose any more time.

STARKEY

Yes, sir!
(To the men)
Stay right here when you're finished. We don't want to lose any more time. And snap it up! Snap it up! We don't want to lose any more time.

(The men move more quickly)

MAJOR

Starkey!

STARKEY

Yes, sir!

MAJOR

This time we'll call the roll immediately. I want to blow Minnesota off the map before someone else does.

STARKEY

Yes, sir!

(To the men)

Okay, finish up, finish up! And then everybody line right up for the roll call. Let's go, men. Let's go.

(The men speed up their activities still further, putting the last things in place, then come together in the assembly area and mill about uncertainly in an attempt to form a line. Starkey approaches with his clipboard)

All set? Then let's begin.

(Bends toward his clipboard)

Henderson!

(There is no answer. Starkey calls out again, still with his head down)

Sergeant Henderson!

(Again there is no answer. This time, a few of the men begin looking around among themselves, searching for Henderson. Starkey speaks again, more loudly than before and with growing irritation)

Henderson, goddam it—why the hell don't you . . . answer . . . when . . .

(Starkey advances in anger toward the men, then stops and his voice trails away when he does not see Henderson among them. Puzzled, Starkey scans the group of men, looking for Henderson, but he does not find him; for Henderson, while the set was being assembled, has slipped away behind a piece of the scenery; and hopefully, he has done this without being noticed by the audience)

Where is he?

(The men stare at each other in confusion and re-

act with surprise when they realize that Henderson
is not there among them)

JOE

He ain't here, I guess.

(The Major approaches impatiently)

MAJOR

What's wrong?

STARKEY

Henderson isn't here.

MAJOR

Why isn't he?
(As he gets no answer)
He's supposed to be here.

STARKEY

Well, he isn't.

MAJOR

Then go get him. What do you mean he isn't here? Find
him. Fast. You, you.
(The Major points to Fisher and Joe. Each darts
offstage in a different direction calling Henderson's
name)
He *has* to be here. We can't go ahead without him. He's
got to die now on the takeoff for Minnesota.

(Fisher returns, then Joe)

FISHER

He didn't answer me.

JOE

I don't see him.

MAJOR

Dammit, I'll kill him! Where is he?

JOE

(Serious)
Maybe he went A.W.O.L.

(Bailey starts to laugh)

MAJOR

There's nothing funny about this!
(Shouts toward the wings)
Hey, Bill! Hey, Ron!
(The Sportsmen enter quickly in their M.P. uniforms, one carrying his golf club, the other carrying
his shotgun. There is about them now an air of
inexorable competence, as though they have learned
very quickly all the things they are supposed to
be doing)
That sergeant is missing. Henderson. Have you seen him?
(Both shake their heads)
Lock all the doors back there and find him. Get him back
here. As fast as you can.

BOTH

O—kay!

(The Sportsmen throw quick salutes and hurry
off in opposite directions. The Major strides about
furiously)

MAJOR

This is a hell of a time—a *hell* of a time for one of you people to start cutting up.

JOE

(Dejectedly, after a few seconds of silence)
I hope he never comes back.

MAJOR

(Surprised)
What?

JOE

I said—I'm sorry.

MAJOR

What *did* you say?

JOE

I said, I hope he never comes back.

MAJOR

Who asked you?

JOE

You did, sir. You just asked me—

MAJOR

I mean who asked you in the first place?

JOE

(Shrugs)
I'm sorry, sir.

MAJOR

(Suddenly curious)
Why do you hope he never comes back?

JOE

I just don't think I want to die yet either. I'd sooner stop
now, while I'm still alive, even though I am only a Pfc.

MAJOR

Well, we *can't* stop now. Right here in the middle—just
like that. And someone has to get killed.

FISHER

Can I get killed, instead?

MAJOR

No, not yet. I need you for later.

YOUNG FISHER

How about me?

BAILEY

(Enviously)
That's not fair, sir! He just got here.

JOE

Yeah. Why should he be the one? He doesn't even have
any experience.

YOUNG FISHER

I could do it, sir. Really, I could. I can get killed now, if
you'll only give me a chance.

MAJOR

No, I'm afraid they're right. You're still a little too new.

BAILEY

Good!

MAJOR

But, Bailey. Aaaah, Bailey! My favorite soldier. You've been here a *long* time, haven't you? You want to be promoted, don't you? You wanted to replace Henderson, didn't you? How would you like to be a sergeant now, right now? Why not?

BAILEY

Oh no, sir. No thank you, sir. I want to replace Henderson *after* he's killed, like I'm supposed to. Not before. I mean that, Major.

(The Major moves about a bit in frustration and then addresses all the men)

MAJOR

You want to go ahead, don't you?
(The men receive the question in stubborn silence. They would just as soon stop)
We can't just sit here now and do nothing, can we?

(There is no reply for several seconds)

FISHER

Can we go home then?

MAJOR

No, you can't go home.

JOE

Can I go on furlough? I've got lots of leave coming to me.

MAJOR

No, you can't go on furlough, not now.

JOE

When then?

MAJOR

After the mission.

JOE

I get killed on the mission.

MAJOR

Then you won't need the furlough.

JOE

I want my furlough.

MAJOR

(Shouting out into the theater in exasperation)
Where's Henderson?
(There is no response)
Dammit—I'll blast him apart!

BAILEY

Can we go to our dressing rooms and wait?

MAJOR

No! You can wait right here!
(To Starkey)
We have to do *something!*

STARKEY

We could close the curtains now and have an intermission.

MAJOR

(Shouts)

Yes, close the curtains. But no intermission.

(To the men as the curtains start to close and the
lights dim)

Stay where you are, all of you. I want all of you locked
in right where you are. Just wait till I find Henderson.
Then I'll show you all something. Starkey, you can come
with me.

(Starkey comes forward and joins the Major down-
stage just before the curtain closes behind him)

MAJOR

(Almost as though aloud to himself)

They've got to be watched. I never really trust them. I
bet they're lounging around and complaining right now.
I'll bet they're even smoking. They've always got to be
watched.

STARKEY

Should I go back and watch them?

MAJOR

I want you to find Henderson.

STARKEY

Suppose he's already gone?

MAJOR

(Tiredly, and with a touch of sadness)

139

He has to be somewhere. Sooner or later, everyone is found. Sooner or later everyone is caught. Even me.

STARKEY

You?

MAJOR

Yes. Find Henderson. I'm tired. I work very hard, too.

STARKEY

I never heard you talk this way.

MAJOR

That's because you never listen. You're always so busy with your wife and your donuts.

STARKEY

I do my job, don't I?

MAJOR

You do it very well. Go find Henderson.

STARKEY

What will you do with him?

MAJOR

I'm gonna kill him.

STARKEY

No, I mean it.

MAJOR

So do I. I'm going to kill him.

STARKEY

You can't *kill* him, really.

140

MAJOR

Why not?

STARKEY

Are you kidding?

MAJOR

Are you?

STARKEY

You can't just kill people.

MAJOR

Why not?

STARKEY

Because you just—well, can't.

MAJOR

And just what do you think we've been doing?

(For a moment, Starkey is stunned. He responds softly, in a tone of deep bewilderment)

STARKEY

Are you crazy? Who do you think you are?

MAJOR

Who do *you* think I am?
(Turning away, as Starkey doesn't answer)
Go find Henderson so I can kill him and get it over with.

STARKEY

You really think you're going to kill him?

MAJOR

If I have to.

STARKEY

Right here? Right out in front of all these people? In front of all these witnesses?

MAJOR

If I have to.

STARKEY

Oh, no. They won't let you. They won't just sit there and let you kill him.

MAJOR

Yes, they will.

STARKEY

Listen. Do you mean it when you say that?

MAJOR

Do *you* mean it when you ask that?

STARKEY

Oh, God! Why won't you ever answer a question?

MAJOR

(Taunting him)
Why won't you?

STARKEY

Goddammit, are you trying to make a fool out of me now ... out here ... with everyone watching?

MAJOR

Don't shout at me.

STARKEY

I'm sorry.

MAJOR

Don't swear at me.

STARKEY

I'm sorry.

MAJOR

Don't contradict me.

STARKEY

I'm sorry.

MAJOR

And don't challenge my authority.

STARKEY

I'm sorry. I am sorry, but . . . may I ask a question?

MAJOR

Oh, go ahead.

STARKEY

Are you acting now? Or do you really mean everything you're saying?

MAJOR

It doesn't matter. Can't you see that? All that does matter is what happens. That's the thing you don't realize. And that's the reason you're always so aimless and wishy-washy in just about everything you do.

STARKEY

Hey, wait a minute! You start talking that way to me and I'll quit, too.

MAJOR

No, you won't quit. You haven't got the character to quit. Popping off in front of a lot of people like this is just about as far as you'll ever go.

STARKEY

Don't you be so sure.

MAJOR

I am sure. Quit, if you think you can. Go ahead, quit.

STARKEY

I quit!

(Starkey starts away, while the Major watches confidently. Starkey slows after a few steps, hesitates, and comes to a stop, hanging his head with shame)

MAJOR

No, you won't quit. You're a captain, and captains don't quit. Captains obey. You're conditioned to agree and you're trained to do as you're told. You like the pay and the prestige, and you do enjoy your job here, remember? So you'll stay right where you are, do just what you're supposed to, and continue reciting your lines exactly on cue—just as you're doing right now.

STARKEY

No, I'm not! I am not! Goddammit, I'm not!

MAJOR

Yes, you are. Should I show you?

(He holds up the script and offers to open it)

You can shout it out to them even louder one more time, if it makes you feel so free, and honest, and independent. But after that, you will have to go on saying and doing exactly what you're supposed to, because *that's* what you are—let's face it—that's *all* you are, a captain. And also, because you're afraid of this.

(Holds up his hand, his fingers outstretched)

Do you know what this is?

STARKEY

A hand.

MAJOR

No.

(Bending his fingers to clench them)

It's a fist. You're afraid it can smash you to bits, and it can. And you also know that I can summon a whole army of people with guns and clubs just by blowing on this marvelous little military whistle of mine.

(The Major reaches into his pocket, pulls out his baby pacifier, and begins munching on it. Starkey laughs)

STARKEY

That's not a whistle. It's a baby's pacifier.

MAJOR

It's a whistle, if I say it is. And if I do say it is, do you know what you'd better say?

STARKEY

(Capitulating, after a moment)
Yes, sir.

MAJOR

What do you say?

STARKEY

Yes, sir.

MAJOR

It's a whistle.

STARKEY

Yes, sir.

MAJOR

Good. Find Henderson and bring him to me.

STARKEY

Yes, sir.

(The Major has won and is satisfied, and his air
of antagonism leaves him. He speaks in a tone that
is suddenly soft and almost apologetic, appealing
to Starkey for understanding and forgiveness)

MAJOR

My friend—I really don't want to talk to you this way.

STARKEY

(Surprised)
No?

MAJOR

But I must. Do you understand?

STARKEY

Yes, sir.

MAJOR

Thank you.

(The Major leaves, carrying his script. Starkey stares after him with resentment)

STARKEY

(Sardonically)
Yes, sir.
(He turns and shuffles forward a step or two to address the audience)
  I am a man.
  I'm not a thing.
  I'm a modern, contemporary, adult human being.
  I'm a very decent and respectable and sensitive
    human being.
  I'm married now, and I work for a living, just like
    you—you all know that.
  I've got pride and character and dignity, and I
    have a wish and a determination to maintain my
    self-respect.
  I do have convictions.
  I have very deep convictions and very genuine and
    powerful feelings that I want to give voice to
    in loud, rolling sentences like: "Was this the
    face that launched a thousand ships and burnt
    the topless towers of Iliom? Sweet Helen,
    make me immortal with a kiss."

(With a wishful smile)
    I want to make long speeches like that.
(With even greater longing)
    I want to play tragedy.
(Turning grave again)
      That's why I'm really not so happy here right now.
      The part I have is too . . . limited.
      I'm not sure I like it here any more,
      Squeezed in between the curtain
      And the edge of the stage,
      Squeezed into this small narrow role,
      Pressed into a tight uniform,
      Between the curtain
      And the edge of the stage,
      And forced to say,
      "Yes, sir."

(Starkey turns bitterly and starts to walk offstage. He comes to a stop at a sharp, frightening sound from behind the curtain—three raps on a door as loud and sharp as gunshots, then three more. From behind the curtain Ruth's voice is heard, shrill and quavering with terror, answered by the voices of two men, who alternate in their responses)

RUTH

Go away!

MAN'S VOICE

Is he in there?

RUTH

Go away!

148

MAN'S VOICE

Is he in there?

(Starkey looks through the curtain, then hurries offstage in fright, while the curtain opens slowly and the conversation in back of it continues.

The curtain opens on Ruth in her dressing room, which has been set inside the briefing room. There is a closet, a mirror, a stool, and a make-up table. Ruth is in a state of panic as she tries frantically to slip a jacket on over her blouse and pack some of her things in a small traveling case. She is shouting toward the door; and the voices of the two men are replying from outside)

RUTH

What do you want?

MAN'S VOICE

Have you seen him?

RUTH

Leave me alone!

VOICE

We want to find him.

RUTH

He isn't here!

VOICE

Have you seen him?

RUTH

Leave me alone!

VOICE

We'll be back.

RUTH

He isn't here!

VOICE

We'll be back.

RUTH

No—leave me alone! Oh, God! God, keep them away!
 (Ruth shakes so violently that she can scarcely
 fasten the buttons of her suit. As she moves to the
 traveling case, three knocks sound softly on the
 door. Ruth shudders with alarm and cries out
 hysterically)
Go away! Go away!

 (The door opens and Starkey looks in with surprise and enters)

STARKEY

Hey, let me in. What's the matter, honey?
 (Ruth collapses against him, hugging and kissing
 him with relief)
Oh, Jesus, darling, it's you! It's you, it's you. I'm so
glad! I'm so scared!

STARKEY

Easy, honey, easy. What are you scared of?

RUTH

Them.

STARKEY

Who?

RUTH

I don't know. They're after someone. Every few seconds
they come here and—
    (The three knocks thunder at the door again, then
    the second three)
You see?

VOICE

Where is he?

RUTH

I don't know! I tell you, I don't know!

STARKEY

    (To Ruth)
Who?

RUTH

    (To Starkey)
I don't know.

VOICE

Have you seen him yet?

RUTH

Go away.

VOICE

Is he in there yet?

RUTH

Go away!

VOICE

We'll be back.

RUTH

Go to hell!

STARKEY

Calm down, baby. Don't fall apart.

RUTH

Let's get out of this place . . . *please!* Something terrible is happening—I just know it is.

STARKEY

Nothing's happening. They're just looking around—

RUTH

They're waiting outside, to knock again. They're not looking anywhere.

STARKEY

You're a little crazy, darling. Do you know that?

RUTH

Oh, God—I know who they're after! They're after *us*.

STARKEY

Oh, come on. You *are* a little crazy, aren't you?

(Starkey tries to comfort her with an embrace. But Ruth pulls away)

RUTH

It's true. That's why they keep coming here. They're after
us! Every few seconds—
(The three knocks sound on the door again, a bit
softer and slower than before, then the second
three)
You see?

VOICE

Where is he?

STARKEY

(Calling out)
Who?

VOICE

Is that a man in there?

STARKEY

Yeah. What the hell do you want?

(Starkey moves to the door and yanks it open. The
two Sportsmen are outside. They push their heads
in, amiably and inquisitively, and enter casually)

GOLFER

Oh, hi!

HUNTER

Hiyah, Captain. Good to see you.

STARKEY

What's going on?

GOLFER

We're trying to find that sergeant.

153

HUNTER

Henderson. The one that's missing.

STARKEY

Why do you keep coming here?

GOLFER

We don't keep coming here.

HUNTER

We've got to look everywhere.

GOLFER

Until we find him.

HUNTER

He's not in here, is he?

STARKEY

I'm in here.

HUNTER

Oh, sure. I forgot. Sorry to disturb you.

GOLFER

We're just looking around now.
     (Glances at his wrist watch)
You'll let us know when you see him, won't you?

GOLFER

     (With confidence)
Sure, don't worry. He'll let us know. So long, Captain.

154

HUNTER

See you later.

(Both wave good-bye, smiling genially, and close the door)

STARKEY

See? It's just those two characters the Major worked in.

RUTH

They'll be back. Didn't you hear them? They said they'll see you later.

STARKEY

So what? There's nothing to be afraid of.

RUTH

That's what you say. Darling, let's get out of here. *Now!* Something's gone wrong—I just know it has. I want to get out of here while we still can.

STARKEY

Nothing's gone wrong.

RUTH

Then what are you doing in here now? Why do they keep knocking at my door? Why aren't you out there somewhere, flying that stupid mission to Minnesota like you're supposed to?

STARKEY

Henderson copped out. He's disappeared.

RUTH

Good for him. I'm quitting, too.

STARKEY

What do you mean, *you're* quitting? You're all through, anyway.

RUTH

I'm quitting for good. I mean it. Let's get out of ⸻
  (Name of city in which performance is taking place)
before you blow this place up, too. I've had enough. Really, I have. I'm tired. I'm tired now of always trying to pretend to be somebody I'm not. I'm not sure who or what I really am any more. I'm going to give this all up and do something else.

STARKEY

Like what?

RUTH

I don't know. Maybe I'll *become* a Red Cross girl.

STARKEY

You still can't make coffee.

RUTH

I could learn, if I ever really tried. Couldn't I? Couldn't I learn how to do even that?

STARKEY

  (Cuddling her)
You can do anything, honey. Really, you can. You can be anyone you want to be.

RUTH

  (Pleased)
Really?

STARKEY

Sure. Why, I'll bet you're the best Red Cross girl anyone's ever seen.

RUTH

Ah, cut it out.
(She kisses him, grateful for the compliment, then
takes his face in her hands and turns solemn)
Darling—help me. I want to go.

STARKEY

You're silly.
(He kisses her and holds her close)
Where's that great sense of humor of yours? In the old days, you'd have had something funny to say about that crazy knocking on the door.

RUTH

There's really nothing funny about it.
(The three knocks sound again, then the second
three, softer and slower than before. Ruth jerks
away at the first sound and speaks in a small
scream)
You see?

VOICE

Where is he?
(Starkey strides angrily to the door)

RUTH

What do you want from me?

VOICE

Is he in there yet?

(Starkey pulls open the door and confronts the two Sportsmen again. They enter calmly, still smiling, but their manner is more purposeful and deliberate now than earlier)

STARKEY

What the hell are you two doing?

HUNTER

Oh, hi.

GOLFER

Have you got him yet?

STARKEY

No, I haven't got him.

HUNTER

We're still looking for him.

GOLFER

That's what we're doing.

(Starkey and the two Sportsmen converse now as though understanding each other perfectly, without urgency or alarm)

STARKEY

Well, don't come back here. I'll be here. I'm in charge here.

HUNTER

If you see him—

STARKEY

I'll take care of things here.

GOLFER

Oh, that's fine then.
(To the Hunter)
He'll take care of things.

(The Hunter looks at his watch)

HUNTER

See you soon.

(The Sportsmen leave, closing the door. Starkey
heaves a sigh)

STARKEY

You see? There's nothing to worry about now. Is there?
(Despondently, with resignation, Starkey looks at
his own watch. Then, with a stretch of great, ago-
nized reluctance, he moves up in back of Ruth,
places his hands on her shoulders, and speaks suddenly, changing his tone without warning to an
exact and frightening imitation of the voice through
the door)
Where is he?

RUTH

(Startled)
Who?

STARKEY

Is he in here?

RUTH

Who? What are *you* talking about? What do *you* want from me?

STARKEY

You know who. Henderson. The one we're looking for.

RUTH

Oh, no! Not *you!* I can't remember.

STARKEY

Yes, you can, honey. You can do anything. Except tell a good lie. Is he in here—wait, don't answer yet. If you lie, I'll know it. If you tell me he isn't here, I'll know he is. If you tell me you didn't see him, I'll know you did. If you tell me you did, I'll know you didn't, if you tell me he is, I'll know he isn't, so you better tell me the truth.

RUTH

You're saying all this to confuse me.

STARKEY

That's right. And now that I have confused you, I'll ask you again. Sweetheart, *where is he? I've* got to find him!

(Ruth ponders heavily, trying to puzzle out the alternatives, and finally gives up)

RUTH

In my closet.

(Starkey turns from her with relief and moves to the open door of the closet)

STARKEY

(In dry sing-song, facing the closet)
Come out, come out, wherever you are.
(The garments hanging in the closet stir, and
slowly, almost one limb at a time, Henderson
emerges from inside. He is dressed in the casual
clothes that a young professional actor of the time
and the place would be likely to wear on his way to
the theater. He waits in silence, a bit defiantly.
Starkey regards him with a look of wry hostility)
Where'd you get the funny costume?

HENDERSON

They're civilian clothes. They used to be very popular.

STARKEY

What are you doing in—say, just what *are* you doing in
my wife's dressing room?

RUTH

Oh, don't be crazy. I'm old enough to be his mother. Ask
him.

HENDERSON

I'm young enough to be her son.

RUTH

That means you're old enough to be his father.

STARKEY

I'm not his father.

RUTH

Help him anyway.

STARKEY

Help him?

RUTH

Help him get away.

STARKEY

Help *him?*
(To Henderson)
Do you know the kind of trouble you've—

(The three knocks sound suddenly on the door
again, then the second three)

RUTH

(Shrieking)
What do you want?

VOICE

Is he in there yet?

STARKEY

Go away.

VOICE

Who's that?

STARKEY

You know who it is.

VOICE

Have you got him yet?

STARKEY

No. Go away. And leave us alone.

(There is a second or two of silence during which
the three wait tensely)
Do you realize the trouble you're causing? Everything is
stopped. Nobody can do anything. Nobody can go home
and eat their supper and drink their coffee and go to bed,
all because of you. What are you doing here now in those
silly civilian clothes when you're supposed to be out there
bombing Minnesota?

HENDERSON

I'm quitting.

STARKEY

What do you mean you're quitting? Right now? Right in
the middle? Right—

HENDERSON

Right before I have to fly to Minnesota and be killed! Why
should I if I don't want to?

STARKEY

Why shouldn't you if we want you to? It's only make-be-
lieve.

HENDERSON

I don't *want* to make believe any more. I'm tired of playing
soldier—like those two jokers out there. I don't want to
make believe I'm going to be killed. I don't want to make
believe I'm *not* going to be killed. I don't want to make believe I'm killing other people, and then have to make believe I'm not killing them. You know, I don't think I even
want to be an actor any more.
    (With a touch of genuine sorrow)
I just wanna go home.

163

(Pauses humbly)
I want to see my mother again.

STARKEY

(Kindly, but with a trace of scorn)
Do you want your nipple back?

HENDERSON

I just wanna go home.

STARKEY

If we give you medals and more money and promote you
to lieutenant?
        (Henderson shakes his head)
To a captain?
        (Henderson shakes his head again)
You really mean it, don't you?
        (Henderson nods. Starkey gazes at him soberly a
        moment and then sits down helplessly on the stool
        in front of the dressing-room mirror. In wonder-
        ment, he studies his reflection for a few seconds,
        as though trying to figure out who he really is. At
        last, he speaks to Ruth)
What am I supposed to do?

RUTH

Honey, you have to help him—

STARKEY

I'm supposed to find him and bring him back.

RUTH

—you have to help him get away.

164

STARKEY

The doors are locked.

RUTH

You and I can get out, can't we? Maybe we can sneak him out between us.

STARKEY

I can't do that. That's not why I'm here.

RUTH

Yes, you can, darling. That's *just* why you're here.

STARKEY

Goddammit—I'm not the villain around here! I'm not the one who's running things! Am I? *Am I?* I just do what I'm told to do, along with everyone else.
(Ruth and Henderson remain silent, watching him.
Starkey storms about in front of them for a few
moments longer and then gives in)
All right, I'll help him. I'll do what I can. It's not that hard.
I know a safer and easier way.
(To Henderson)
Just go to the Major and tell him you're quitting so he can
get someone to take your place. That's all you have to do.
(As Henderson shakes his head)
Why not?

HENDERSON

You'll laugh.

STARKEY

I'm not doing any more laughing tonight.

165

HENDERSON

I'm afraid.

STARKEY

Of what?

HENDERSON

The Major.

STARKEY

The Major? The Major is almost out of his mind with hysteria. He doesn't know what to do next.

HENDERSON

You tell him for me. I don't want to see him again.

STARKEY

What are you afraid of? He can't make you go if you don't want to.

RUTH

What *can* he do?

STARKEY

Nothing. It's a free country, isn't it?
(To Henderson)
He can get angry and call you a few names. Maybe he can hold back your pay awhile. But that's about all.

HENDERSON

Are you lying now? Or are you telling me the truth? Buddy, I can't tell any more.

STARKEY

I haven't got time to lie. I just want to get things going

smoothly again, without any inconvenience to anybody. Come on back, will you, and make it easier for all of us.

HENDERSON

Will you come with me?

STARKEY

Sure, I will.

RUTH

Will you explain for him?

STARKEY

Sure, I'll explain. I promise I will. I'll take care of you. I'll take care of everything, if you'll just come back now.

(Starkey puts his arm around Henderson's shoulders as he attempts to persuade him. This time, Henderson makes no move to recoil, but stands in silence, deliberating.

The three knocks sound on the door again, softer and slower still. Starkey looks at Henderson, awaiting permission to reply)

What do you say?

HENDERSON

You promise? You promise you'll protect me?

STARKEY

I give you my word.

(Starkey puts his hand out by way of emphasizing his promise, and Henderson shakes it. Henderson nods, giving assent)

Good.

(Starkey sighs with relief, glad that it's over, and calls out toward the door)

STARKEY

Come in. Come on in.

(The Sportsmen enter. They react with grins of affable delight when they see Henderson standing there)

GOLFER

Oh, hi. There you are.

HUNTER

We've been looking all over for you.

STARKEY

You haven't been looking all over. You've been looking here. Take him to the Major and stop dragging things out.

GOLFER

Sure, Captain. Thanks.

(Henderson moves toward the door. He pauses as he comes in front of Starkey)

HENDERSON

Remember—you promised.

STARKEY

I'll be right there.

(Henderson passes close to Ruth. He reaches out and touches her arm gratefully)

HENDERSON

Thanks . . . thank you. You know—
(Attempts an affectionate joke)
—I always even liked your coffee.

(Ruth offers a forced smile of encouragement as
Henderson exits between the two Sportsmen. They
slap Henderson's shoulder in friendly fashion and
leave with cordial waves to Starkey, closing the
door)

RUTH

(Sadly, when she and Starkey are alone)
What's going to happen to him?

STARKEY

Nothing.

RUTH

You're lying, aren't you?

STARKEY

(With sincerity)
No, I'm not.

RUTH

(Sitting down)
I'm going to wait and see.

STARKEY

Go home, Ruth. They've got to take this junk away.
(By "junk," Starkey is referring to the flats and
props that constitute the dressing room. Starkey
snaps his fingers in a signal, and two Idiots appear
out of the surrounding darkness and begin push-
ing the dressing room offstage toward one of the
wings.
Ruth rises to step out of the way. She picks up her
traveling case to take it with her. Starkey reaches

169

for it and puts it back down)
Leave it here. Nothing bad happens to us. The Major
promised me that.

(Doubtfully, Ruth relinquishes the traveling case.
As the dressing room is being removed on one
side, Starkey guides Ruth across stage toward the
other)

RUTH

If this is a trick—

STARKEY

It's not a trick.

RUTH

If you lied to him—

STARKEY

I didn't lie to him.

RUTH

He's just a kid.

STARKEY

I know that.

RUTH

If anything happens to him—

STARKEY

Nothing will happen to him.

RUTH

If anything does happen to him—

STARKEY

(Indulging her)
Yeah?

RUTH

(Quietly, for emphasis)
Don't come home.

(Starkey looks at her with surprise)

STARKEY

Hey! You really mean that, don't you?

RUTH

I just . . . won't want you there.

STARKEY

(In joking reassurance)
Honey—
(He kisses her)
—put a pie in the oven.
(Ruth does not respond to his kiss or his attempt at humor. As Starkey watches, she turns from him grimly and exits.

Starkey shrugs and starts back across the stage. As he walks, the stage is illuminated fully again, and all the men from the preceding scene in the briefing room are revealed sprawling and lounging in that area in which they were last seen. Several smoke cigarettes. They stir attentively as Starkey approaches)
Okay, boys. Let's go. Douse those cigarettes, will you?

(The door to the briefing room opens and Henderson enters with the two Sportsmen. The Sportsmen

are still smiling, and for a moment the three of
them seem to form a close, congenial group. But
suddenly, the Sportsmen seize Henderson by the
arms and fling him into the room roughly, taking
him completely by surprise and sending him top-
pling to the floor. The men react with looks and
exclamations of interest and alarm)

HENDERSON

(Springing up)
Hey, what the hell's the idea?

(Before anyone can speak, the Major enters with a
clenched fist, striding onstage toward Henderson)

MAJOR

I ought to knock your goddam head off!

(Henderson retreats from him a step or two, in fear
and puzzlement)

HENDERSON

Hey, take it easy, will you? Take it easy.

MAJOR

What the hell are you doing here out of uniform?

HENDERSON

I'm quitting. That's what.
    (Motioning toward Starkey)
He'll tell you.

(Starkey takes a doubtful step forward to inter-
vene and musters a very firm voice)

STARKEY

Yes, Major. I told him he—

(The Major pays no attention to Starkey but speaks sternly again to Henderson)

MAJOR

Get back into uniform.

(Henderson motions imploringly toward Starkey again and waits expectantly)

STARKEY

Major. Major, I—

(The Major turns toward Starkey with a look of glaring disapproval)

MAJOR

I ordered him to get back into uniform. Are you going to quarrel with that order?

(Starkey wilts. He steps back, dropping his eyes)

STARKEY

No, sir.

(The Major turns back to Henderson. A moan of disappointment and despair escapes Henderson when he realizes Starkey will not help him and that he now must brave the Major alone)

HENDERSON

I'm not going to.

MAJOR

Henderson, I'm ordering you to get back into your uniform.

HENDERSON

Ordering me? Are you crazy? *Ordering me?* Who do you think you are?

MAJOR

Henderson, I am giving you a direct order. And I am giving you that direct order for the last time.

HENDERSON

I think you're nuts. I'm getting out of here.

MAJOR

Stop him.

HENDERSON

You just try!
(Henderson starts away toward one side. The Golfer bars his way and draws his golf club back menacingly, as though preparing to tee off directly at Henderson. Henderson stops in disbelief)
Hey! What do you think you're gonna—
(Suddenly, the Golfer does swing the club at Henderson murderously. Henderson jumps back and just does elude the head of the club in time. Now the Golfer brandishes the golf club as a weapon and blocks Henderson's path. Incredulous, Henderson starts away in the other direction, approaching the Hunter, who readies his shotgun. Henderson, exclaiming indignantly about the Golfer, is unaware of the Hunter and his gun for the first few seconds)

174

Are you crazy? Did you see what he just did? He tried to kill me with that club. He—

> (Henderson is speaking directly now to the Hunter. He breaks off with increased amazement when he realizes that the Hunter has leveled his shotgun almost right up against his stomach. In bewilderment, he points a childlike finger, as though to ask an innocent question)

Hey, what are you doing with that? Say, mister—*mister*, cut it out, will you? What are—

> (Suddenly, the Hunter pulls the trigger, and the gun goes off with a deafening roar. Henderson is knocked across stage by the blast, emitting a loud, agonized, howling cry. He slams into Starkey and clings to him for a few seconds, screaming again and shuddering violently. His hold weakens and he slides to the floor slowly, leaving a large, bright smear of fresh blood on Starkey's shirtfront. The Golfer watches Henderson alertly, as though ready to bludgeon him should he attempt to rise.
>
> The Major and the two Sportsmen form a silent group as Henderson, on the floor, goes through a protracted death agony, moaning and gasping, shrieking, muttering, shivering, babbling, reaching upward toward nothing once or twice for help, turning, writhing, struggling, giving up at last, sinking flat, and finally, after a waning gasp, lying absolutely still.
>
> For a few seconds, there is complete silence as Henderson lies there, and the men stare down at him mutely in utter horror. Then the Major speaks quietly)

MAJOR

Starkey?

STARKEY

Sir?

MAJOR

(Pointing to Henderson)
Get that junk out of here.

STARKEY

Yes, sir.
(The Sportsmen leave; and the Major moves into
the area of his office, where he stands facing the
blackboard, his back to the men. As soon as they
are gone, Starkey and all the others relax suddenly
from the great tension and break out with sighs and
chuckles of enormous relief. Starkey grins and
laughs also for a few seconds, and then, looking
down at Henderson, begins slowly to applaud the
motionless body)
Very good, kid. I've really got to hand it to you. Oh, boy!
That was really very good.
(Starkey sighs again and turns away to sit down.
He notices that there is no response from Henderson. Starkey seems surprised for a few moments,
then annoyed)
Okay, okay. Don't overdo it. You can get up now. Come
on. Hey!
(Perplexed by the absence of any response from
Henderson, Starkey returns and kneels to shake
him. He turns Henderson over onto his back)
Hey! Move, will you? Let's go now, let's—oh!
(Starkey pulls his hand back from Henderson's
body and stares at his fingers with alarm)

My God! This is blood! This is real blood!
      (Starkey looks closely at Henderson's face and then
      goes rigid with amazement)
He's dead! Hey! He's really dead!

BAILEY

      (Stunned)
N-o-o-o-o!

      (Joe lets out a long, low whistle. Starkey remains
      kneeling beside Henderson's body, as though un-
      able to move)

MAJOR

Starkey?

STARKEY

Sir?

MAJOR

Don't you know?

STARKEY

Yes, sir.
      (To the men, pointing toward Henderson)
He wants us to get this junk out of here.
      (The men stand without moving, still astounded)
Come on. We have to. Bailey . . . Joe.

JOE

I guess we gotta.

      (While Starkey remains kneeling, Joe, Bailey,
      Fisher, Fisher's Kid Brother, and even the Idiots

come forward to help remove Henderson's body from the stage in a slow and somber funeral procession. As Henderson's body is dragged very gently away, the Idiots, surprisingly, straighten and begin singing and moving like normal men. The song is the same Sousa march that was sung earlier by the other men; but now the tone and temper is funereal, and the lines of dialogue that follow are spoken against the background, or in the pauses, of the song)

IDIOTS

(Singing)
"Be kind to your web-footed friends."

BAILEY

(With a bitter glance at the Major)
Let's lug the guts out of here.

IDIOTS

"For a duck may be somebody's mother."

JOE

Who would have thought—Jesus, who would have thought the little bastard had so much blood in him?

IDIOTS

"They live in a stream by the swamp,
Where the weather is always damp."

YOUNG FISHER

(In angry fear, to Fisher)
Hey! I thought you told me nobody got killed here.

FISHER

(Coldly, cruelly, with no hint of an apology toward
his younger brother)
I was lying to you.

(Fisher exits, following the others. His Kid Brother
halts a moment, shaken by the reply, then hurries
out after him with a look of bewilderment. The
song continues from offstage)

IDIOTS

"Now you may think that this is the end.
Well it is."

(Starkey and the Major are left alone. Very softly,
the Major begins whistling the rest of the melodic
line of the song that was terminated so abruptly
by the voices offstage. Starkey remains motionless
and silent for another few seconds)

STARKEY

You really killed him, didn't you?

(The Major replies quietly, almost regretfully)

MAJOR

Do you want the truth? Or do you want a lie?

STARKEY

I didn't know you were going to kill him.

MAJOR

Why should *you* care?

STARKEY

I just didn't know it, that's all.

MAJOR

But what difference does it make, really? Were you so fond
of him? Did you know him so well, or even at all? Was he
anything more to you than just a name? You didn't even
care for him, did you? So what difference does it make
to you really if he lives or if he dies?

STARKEY

No difference.

MAJOR

Of course not. So get me a replacement for him now, will
you? That's your job.

(Starkey stands up slowly)

STARKEY

Okay. Send him in.

MAJOR

(With amused surprise)
I should?

STARKEY

I'm sorry, sir.

MAJOR

I'll get you some help.
(Calls offstage toward the side)
Hey, Ronnie! Billy!

(The door at the rear of the briefing room opens
and the two Sportsmen enter from there, still in
their MP uniforms)

BOTH

Sir?

MAJOR

Help the captain find a replacement, will you?
(To Starkey)
I'll go warm up some planes. All right?

STARKEY

(Yielding)
Yes, sir.

MAJOR

(Mildly)
Don't I even get a salute?

STARKEY

Sure.

(Starkey manages a tired smile and salutes politely)

MAJOR

That's better. Ten minutes, then?

STARKEY

Yes, sir.

(The Major exits into the wing, carrying his manuscript.

Starkey sags a bit after the Major has gone. He shakes his head, as though to rouse himself, and pinches his eyes as though to alleviate an inner pain)

GOLFER

Which one would you like, sir? Have you got a preference?

STARKEY

How many have we got?

HUNTER

We have three hundred names on the list.

STARKEY

(Shrugs)
Send in the first one. Give me half a minute, though.

GOLFER

Yes, sir.

(The Sportsmen exit through the door, closing it
after them. Starkey pokes aimlessly around at his
newspaper, portfolio, and clipboard for a few seconds. Abstractedly, he tries to wipe the bloodstain
from his chest with a crumpled sheet of paper.
From far away, and very faintly, there is heard the
eerie, whistling sound of jet engines starting up;
the noise fades after a few seconds. A quiet knock
sounds on the door. Starkey speaks without looking up)

STARKEY

Come in.

(The door to the briefing room opens, and a young
man we have not seen before—Starkey's son—enters timidly, dressed in the same combat attire worn
by the others, except for flight boots. He is about
nineteen, but so slight and so sad and uncertain

that he seems scarcely older or sturdier than Fisher's Kid Brother. He hesitates a few moments, waiting for Starkey to look up and take notice of him. Finally, the boy breaks the silence and speaks, in a tone of great melancholy, as though knowing already he has been sent there to die)

STARKEY'S SON

Hello . . . pop.

(Starkey stares up in astonishment and comes forward slowly)

STARKEY

What are *you* doing here?

STARKEY'S SON

I'm in the army now.

STARKEY

(With a pained, unnatural smile as though trying to ward off the truth of what is happening now)
Oh, no. *You*? Not you. You can't be. You were only born—
(Looks toward the clock)
—just a little while ago. It seems like—
(He points offstage weakly in the direction he first exited with Ruth)
—just a little while ago.

STARKEY'S SON

I'm nineteen years old now.

STARKEY

It doesn't seem possible.

STARKEY'S SON

What's going to happen to me?

STARKEY

You're going to be killed, son. You're going to go away in an airplane and be killed in an explosion.

STARKEY'S SON

Pop—I don't want to go.

STARKEY

(Musing)

You know, I can't believe it. You were just a little kid the last time I saw you.

STARKEY'S SON

I'm just a little kid now.

STARKEY

It's not my fault.

STARKEY'S SON

What were you doing when all this was happening?

STARKEY

What?

STARKEY'S SON

What were you doing when all this was happening?

STARKEY

My job, I guess.

STARKEY'S SON

Pop, you had nineteen years to save me from this. Why didn't you do something?

STARKEY

It didn't seem possible.

STARKEY'S SON

When I was a little boy, of five, or ten, or fifteen, when I was growing up—you loved me then, didn't you? You must have loved me then! Didn't you know they would take me into the army someday if I just kept growing?

STARKEY

It didn't seem possible.

STARKEY'S SON

And now?

STARKEY

It just doesn't seem possible.

STARKEY'S SON

Pop . . . don't you understand?

STARKEY

(Ruminating aloud, as though in a wistful daze)
You know, it's very funny . . .

STARKEY'S SON

Don't you see? Don't you know?

STARKEY

. . . a little while ago . . . just a little while ago . . .

185

STARKEY'S SON

I don't want to die yet!

STARKEY

. . . I wasn't even married . . .

STARKEY'S SON

I don't want to go!

STARKEY

. . . so it's not my fault.

STARKEY'S SON

It is your fault! What were you doing all this time, when you could have been doing something? Where were you before, after Sinclair disappeared, when mother stood here, right on this stage, and screamed at everyone to stop it, stop it! She did. I know she did. She told me she did.

STARKEY

I was there. I was right here with her.

STARKEY'S SON

Doing what?

STARKEY

(Ashamed)
Smirking. I hid in back of her and I smirked.

STARKEY'S SON

No—you were *working*. You were doing your job, weren't you?

STARKEY

Shut up! You're my son!

STARKEY'S SON

You shut up! You're my father!
  (Pleading with him)
Pop . . . Dad . . . Father . . . Stranger . . . help me.
  (As Starkey remains silent)
If I were still a baby in a baby carriage, and someone
wanted to take me away and kill me, you wouldn't let
them, would you? Are you really going to let them take me
away now and send me out there to be killed?

  (Starkey hesitates a moment longer with a look of
  intense misery, and then shakes his head emphati-
  cally)

STARKEY

No! No! I'm not going to!

STARKEY'S SON

Oh, pop, pop! Thanks!

STARKEY

I'm going to get you out of here! I'm going to let you es-
cape! You get away now. Hurry, hurry!
  (As the boy starts toward the door)
No, not that way!
  (Starkey looks about frantically in all directions,
  even out into the theater for an instant, and then
  points offstage to the side opposite the one taken by
  the Major)
This way! Run, run!

  (Starkey's son exits hurriedly. Starkey pauses a

187

moment to pull himself together. The noise of jet
engines starts up again, closer than before. Starkey
looks at his watch, then hurries toward the door,
calling out)

STARKEY

Corporals! Sergeants! Ronnie! Billy! Whoever the hell
you are!
(The door opens and the Sportsmen look in. The
Hunter carries a sheaf of papers)
Send in the next one.

GOLFER

What happened to the first one?

STARKEY

He wasn't good enough. Who's next?

HUNTER

(Reading from list)
Brandwine.

STARKEY

Send in Brandwine.

HUNTER

Yes, sir.

GOLFER

(Calls to someone outside the door)
Hey, you! Yes, you. You're the one. Get in here.

(The Sportsmen stand aside to make room for a
young soldier to enter. It is Starkey's son. He is as

grave and sad as when he entered the first time; he looks almost completely resigned. The Sportsmen exit, shutting the door)

STARKEY

What are *you* doing back here?

STARKEY'S SON

They were waiting for me. They caught me. They told me I had to come back in here and be killed.

STARKEY

It's a mistake. You don't have to.

STARKEY'S SON

It's not a mistake. It's just too late now.

STARKEY

It's not too late. *I* can save you! I can help you get away! Go out the window this time. Don't let anyone catch you. If they try to stop you, tell them you're my son. Tell them you're *my* son and I said it's okay.

(Starkey hurries with the boy to the window, and the boy climbs out. Starkey calls out toward the door)

Billy! Ronnie! Hurry!

(The door opens and the Sportsmen return)

Who's next on the list? He was no good, either.

HUNTER

Mendoza.

STARKEY

Mendoza! Yes, that's the one I want! Mendoza. Send in Mendoza.

GOLFER

(Calling to someone outside the door)
Mendoza! Mendoza! Come on. Come inside.

(As Starkey stares at the open door and waits, the
Major enters slowly from the side, materializing
from the wings with his manuscript. He wears a
knowing, solemn look; his voice is soft and almost
compassionate)

MAJOR

Starkey?
(As Starkey turns)
Hurry up, please. It's time.

STARKEY

I've got him coming in right now.
(Calling toward the open door)
Mendoza! Where is—
(The Sportsmen stand aside to admit another
young soldier. It is Starkey's son again. He stands
at attention in despondent silence as the door closes
behind him and gives not the slightest sign of rec-
ognition. Starkey reacts with shock and dismay
when he sees him. Finally, Starkey turns slowly
toward the Major with a look of mournful compre-
hension)
It's just no use, is it?
(As the Major shakes his head)
Major! They've got three hundred names on that list.

MAJOR

They all belong to him.

(Starkey turns from the Major and looks at the boy closely)

STARKEY

Do you know who I am?

STARKEY'S SON

Yes, sir. You're the captain.

STARKEY

Do you know why you're here?

STARKEY'S SON

They want me to go into an airplane and be killed. You're the one that's going to send me.

STARKEY

And you'll go?

STARKEY'S SON

If I have to.

STARKEY

What's your name, son?

STARKEY'S SON

(With a trace of bitterness)
Son.

(Starkey pulls back from him, wincing with grief, and addresses the Major)

STARKEY

Does he have to go?

(The Major nods and glances at the clock on the wall)

MAJOR

Yes, he does. It's about time. I told you that once.

STARKEY

(To the boy)
You have to go.

STARKEY'S SON

Then will you get angry now? Will you at least raise your voice? Won't you do anything to save me? Won't you do something to show you even care?

STARKEY

Like what?

STARKEY'S SON

(Surprised)
Like what?
(Indicating the Major)
Smash his face.
(Starkey is surprised by the suggestion, then appalled. He turns to stare at the Major, who is right in front of him, as though weighing the possibility. The Major waits without flinching, as though daring him to do something, and for a few seconds the two men look at each other in tense silence, while the boy watches hopefully. The boy cries out again)
Smash it . . . *please*!

(Starkey stares at the Major a few moments longer.
. . . and does nothing. And then, when it is clear

that Starkey intends to do nothing, the Major shakes his head, giving Starkey the signal he needs and the boy his answer.

Starkey turns back to his son, shaking his own head)

STARKEY

No.

STARKEY'S SON

Then will you throw a stone or break a window or let . . . out . . . a . . . scream? Pop, they're going to kill me! Don't you understand that? They are really going to kill me.

(As Starkey shrugs helplessly and continues shaking his head)

Must I really go out now and be killed?

STARKEY

(To the Major)

Must I really send him out now to be killed?

(The Major nods. Starkey turns back to the boy)

You see? It's not my fault.

STARKEY'S SON

Then will you gnash your teeth?

STARKEY

What?

STARKEY'S SON

Will you gnash your teeth? Will you at least do something as old-fashioned as that? Will you beat your chest with your fists and tear your hair? Will you weep for me?

STARKEY

I will weep for you. I promise you that.

STARKEY'S SON

When King David was told that his son had been killed, even in a rebellion against him, he cried: "O my son Absalom! My son, my son Absalom! Would God I had died for thee!"

STARKEY

I will weep for you. I will cry: "My son, my son! Would God I had died for thee!"

STARKEY'S SON

But will you mean it?

STARKEY

(Slowly, with shame)
I won't know. I won't ever really know.

MAJOR

It's time now.

STARKEY'S SON

I'll go.

(Starkey approaches his son as though to embrace him. His son watches him stonily, and Starkey comes to a stop and lets his hands drop awkwardly without touching him)

STARKEY

Good-bye . . . son.

STARKEY'S SON

Bastard!

(Starkey's son turns finally and follows the Major out. The door closes behind them.

Left by himself, Starkey gazes after him sorrow-
fully for a few seconds. The noise of the jet planes
picks up again; they are taking off. Suddenly,
Starkey seems to grow aware of the audience
watching him. He fidgets uncomfortably, as though
realizing he has been observed committing some
dreadful act, and he comes forward guiltily in an
effort to explain)

STARKEY

(To the audience)
Now, none of this, of course, is really happening. It's a
show, a play in a theater, and I'm not really a captain.
I'm an actor.
(His voice rises with emotion, as though to drown
out the noise of a plane that passes very close and
recedes steadily into the distance)
I'm _____ _____.
(He mentions his real name)
You all know that. Do you think that I, _____ _____,
(Repeats his real name)
would actually let my son go off to a war and be killed . . .
and just stand here talking to you and do nothing?
(An edge of hysteria and grief comes into his voice,
as though he knows what is to follow)
Of course not! There is no war taking place here ri—
(In the distance, there is the sound of a single,
great explosion, and Starkey whimpers and seems
on the verge of weeping as he shouts out in-
sistently)
There is no war taking place here now!
(He sags a moment, then continues desperately)
There has never been a war. There never will be a war.
Nobody has been killed here tonight. It's only . . . make-

believe . . . it's a story . . . a show.
> (Bitterly, sarcastically, as though giving up the attempt to persuade the audience—and himself—that what he is saying is true)

Nobody has ever been killed.
> (He shrugs and looks about and then speaks ruefully, as though remembering Ruth's last words to him)

I'm going home now.
> (He takes up his portfolio and his folded newspaper and prepares to leave)

In a few minutes, ushers will pass among you collecting money for the Will Rogers Tuberculosis Sanitarium in Lake Saranac, New York.
> (With irony, a broken man)

Give generously.

> (He starts away slowly, departing in the direction from which he first entered, carrying his portfolio and his folded copy of *The New York Times*, a solitary working man on the way home, his job, for this occasion, done)

THE END